Praise for
PLAY TO WIN!

❝One of contemporary life's great tour guides. Play to Win! sets out clearly, simply, and powerfully a model for life . . . and work. Without question, this cultural change more than any other single item is responsible for the tremendous success British Airways has enjoyed in the U.S. in the past few years.❞

Dale Moss
Executive Vice President
British Airways

❝Play to Win! *is compelling and readable. Individuals and teams in organizations that take these ideas seriously stand to improve not only the quality of their experience at work, but their performance as well. I am thrilled to discover that Larry and Hersch have written it all down at last!*❞

Amy Edmondson, Ph.D.
Assistant Professor of Business
**   Administration, Harvard University**
Coauthor of *Organizational Learning and*
**   *Competitive Advantage***

❝In today's hyper-competitive world, if you aren't playing to win you're bound to lose. Larry and Hersch have redefined winning in a way that allows all of us to relook at our lives and work and discover new ways of getting better results. Citibankers all over the world are benefiting from the ideas in this book. Play to win yourself reading this book and making your life better.❞

Bill Campbell
Executive Vice President
Citibank

66In our company, like most others, winning is essential. This is especially true in the way 'winning' has been redefined by Larry and Hersch. Helping our people become their best and defeat fear is our greatest challenge as leaders. This book shows the way.**99**

Marilyn Neal
Senior Vice President Sales
GTE Directories

66Larry and Hersch Wilson have done a masterful job of helping people understand and apply the powerful principles of cognitive psychology. I recommend it wholeheartedly.**99**

Maxie Maultsby, M.D.
Professor of Psychiatry
Howard University
Author of *Coping Better*

66Anyone can use Play to Win! *to live a more successful and fulfilled life. Packed with answers to help create positive results, you'll find something fresh and valuable with each reading.***99**

Linda Baker
Director of SW CBC
Quaker Oats

66When I went through the Pecos River Play to Win^{SM} program the 'aha!' was immense. This book can change how you think about yourself, your family relationships, and your role as a leader. Keep it at your side for the rest of your life.**99**

Bob Page
President
Quick Chek Food Stores

66_Shows us how to get out of the 'playing not to lose' trap and helps us to learn, grow, create, collaborate—to thrive in life. It really works._**99**

Patricia Harper-Murrah
Assistant Vice President
Associates Commercial Corporation

66Play to Win! _captures the essence of how to change the way you see things so you can dramatically and immediately improve the way you do things. The ideas in_ Play to Win _were a significant part of helping us become one of Fortune Magazine's 'Top 100 companies to work for in 2003.'_**99**

Charlie Eitel
CEO
The Simmons Company

PLAY TO WIN!

ALSO BY

Larry Wilson and Hersch Wilson

STOP SELLING, START PARTNERING

CHANGING THE GAME
The New Way to Sell

Larry Wilson and Spencer Johnson

THE ONE MINUTE SALES PERSON

CHOOSING GROWTH OVER FEAR
IN WORK AND LIFE

PLAY TO WIN!

LARRY WILSON
HERSCH WILSON

Foreword by Ken Blanchard

Bard
Press

AUSTIN, TEXAS

PLAY TO WIN!
Choosing Growth over Fear in Work and Life
Larry Wilson and Hersch Wilson

Bard Press
5275 McCormick Mountain Drive
Austin, Texas 78734
Phone: 512-266-2112   Fax: 512-266-2749
ray@bardpress.com
www.bardpress.com

Pecos River® Division Aon Consulting, Inc.
U.S. Phone: 1-800-PecosRiver
Outside the U.S. 781-861-1700
www.pecosriver.com

Ordering Information
To order additional copies, contact your local bookstore
or visit www.thegreatgameoflife.com
Quantity discounts are available.
Call 941-964-3017

ISBN 1-885167-61-X (paperback)

Library of Congress Cataloging-in-Publication Data
Wilson, Larry
    Play to Win! : choosing growth over fear in work and life / Larry
Wilson, Hersch Wilson : foreword by Ken Blanchard. — 1st ed.
        p.   cm.
    Includes bibliographical references and index.
    ISBN 1-885167-31-8 (hardover)
    1. Wilson, Hersch.   II. Title.
    BF637.S8W528   1998
    158.1—dc21   98-15293

Credits

Executive editor: Leslie Stephen	*Word processing:* Creative Computer Network
Art director/Design: Suzanne Pustejovsky	*Composition:* Round Rock Graphics
Copyeditor: Kathy Bork	*Proofreaders:* Kathy Bork, Deborah Costenbader,
Index: Linda Webster	Doreen Piano

Hardcover Edition
First printing, June 1998
Second printing, May 1999
Third printing, March 2000
Fourth printing, May 2001

Fifth printing, April 2004

Trade Paperback Edition
First printing, August 2004

This book is dedicated
in loving memory to
Bill Payne,
who passed away in July 1997.
Bill was the heart and spirit
of all we stand for
at Pecos River.
He was taken from us too soon
in his journey,
but his spirit lives on
in everything we do.
God bless.

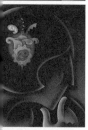

CONTENTS

About the Authors   xiii

Foreword by Ken Blanchard   xv

First Words   xix

Notes from the Authors   xxiii

PART I	3

THE ADVENTURE

1   The Adventure of Your Life   9

PART II	19

RETHINKING THE GAME

2   Redefining Winning and Losing   21

3   Rethinking Success   29

PART III	37

THINKING DIFFERENTLY ABOUT THINKING

4   I Cannot Fail, I Can Only Learn and Grow   41

5   It's All about Results   49

6   The Snake Made Me Do It!   55

7   The Truth Defined   63

8   You Graduated from MSU   69

PART IV	79

SOLVING PROBLEMS AND CREATING RESULTS

9   Stop, Challenge, and Choose!   83

10   The Two-Minute Drill   91

11 "A Little Thing Happens and
the Drama Unfolds"   103

12 The End of Life As We Know It   111

| PART V | 121 |

WORK AND LIFE STRATEGIES

13 The Hero's Journey   125

14 I've Got Your Name in My Pocket   133

15 The Four Fatal Fears   139

16 Playing Not to Lose   147

17 Choosing Growth   155

18 You Bet Your Life!   167

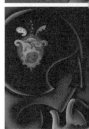

| PART VI | 175 |

THE SPIRITUAL ADVENTURE

19 Spiritual Beings on a Human Path   183

20 Loving Service   193

21 You Are Here to Do Important Work   201

| PART VII | 211 |

CHOOSING GROWTH

22 Six Steps to an Optimal Future   215

23 Deeply Prepared People Create
Their Own Weather   225

Notes   233

Sources   234

Index   238

Photo by Julie Dean, Santa Fe

Larry Wilson is a world-renowned entrepreneur, speaker, and facilitator. The founder of Wilson Learning Corporation and Pecos River Learning Centers, he has three best-selling books to his credit, including *The One Minute Sales Person* (Morrow). Twice having flunked retirement, Larry is currently President of Larry Wilson & Associates. He spends the bulk of his time creating new learning models and curriculum as a way to help organizations grow their people. He lives in Florida.

Hersch Wilson continues to lead Senior Executive teams around the world in rediscovering their courage and creativity while helping those they lead do the same. His clients have included top teams from Eastman Kodak, DuPont, Kraft Foods, Philip Morris, Baxter Healthcare, Genentech, IBM Japan, Aetna, and Ford. He lives in Santa Fe.

Besides collaborating on *Play to Win!* Larry and Hersch have coauthored two best-sellers on sales, *Changing the Game: The New Way to Sell* (Simon & Schuster) and *Stop Selling, Start Partnering* (Wiley), as well as a break-through book on management strategy, *Changing the Game Together: Inventing the Company That Will Put You Out of Business.*

Foreword

By Ken Blanchard

I N 1979, I HEARD A YOUNG AND DYNAMIC SPEAKER talk to an audience of business leaders from the Young Presidents' Organization (YPO). The "ABC's of Personal Power" was an intense and entertaining hour on how to play to win—to go for it—in work and in life. It was a powerful speech and the audience was held spellbound not only by the passion of the speaker but also by the potency of his ideas. The speaker was Larry Wilson.

Larry and I have since shared the speaker's platform all over the world. He continues to be a powerful, dynamic, and wise presence on the dais. I admire him principally because his life's work has been to help individuals

grasp the significance of their lives and to use their courage and creativity to face challenges, handle adversity, and grow as individuals.

It has been in the last fifteen years, as the founder and driving
force of Pecos River Change Management, that Larry's message has
really caught fire. He has the ability to look straight into the eyes
and souls of people—from CEOs of some of our largest institutions
to people who have spent their working lives on factory floors. He
often asks them the same questions: What is your life about? How
are you making the world a better place? What will your legacy be?

These are the questions that, in our "permanent whitewater"
world, we often neglect. We are so busy being busy that we don't
take the time to reflect on and ask the questions that can reshape
our lives. As a result, all around us people are arriving at their
deaths, at the end of their adventure, unfulfilled, lost, and wondering what could have been . . . and it doesn't matter a whit at that
moment whether they were a CEO or a factory worker.

So Larry asks the simple but profound questions and, as important, he has developed a way of thinking and a way of working and
living that can get us closer to the answers. It is called Play to Win.

What an odd phrase. Life certainly isn't about playing, and yet
if you watch children play, beyond the fun they're having you see
intensity, focus, learning, and relating. Life is certainly more than
defeating others—the commonly accepted criterion of winning—it
is about going as far as you can, using up everything that you've
been given to live a full and meaningful life.

Play to Win! is a guide to doing all of that: to living with meaning, passion, and purpose and doing it in a way that resembles children at play—intensely, while learning, having fun, and relating to
the other "kids."

The "playground," if you will, that most of us have chosen is the
world of work, of business, of professions, of "what we do." Helping
you thrive in that playground is one of the important elements of
Play to Win! And, of course, if you are thinking about how you are
going to thrive at work, how you are going to continually change,

adjust, and adapt as we rapidly move deeper into the unknown of the information revolution—read this book! Otherwise you might quickly get left behind.

Why?

Look around! The companies we work for are reinventing themselves as we move from the industrial era to something else. In the very same way, we need to reinvent ourselves. We need to become something different from the employees of another era who checked their brains and their passion at the gate and became solely "hired hands." To be continually successful in the new era will require us, whether we are employees or entrepreneurs, to use all of our creativity, intellectual ability, and courage. We will each need to play to win "to go as far as we can using all that we have and learning from our experience."

In this paradoxical time of great opportunity and no job security, it is the people who understand and grasp this that have a shot at being successful and fulfilled in all aspects of their lives.

Play to Win! will give you the insights and the tools to be better able to deal successfully with permanent whitewater. The ideas are simply presented, easy to use, and can make a profound difference in your life and work. This book is potentially life changing. The philosophy of *Play to Win!*—going as far as you can with all that you have and learning from whatever happens—the consummate thinking strategy for anyone who wants to achieve high performance and fulfillment against the background of our wild and woolly times.

I'm excited by this book and by the potential it creates for thousands of readers. It represents the distillation of thirty years of work, thinking, and creation in the pursuit of helping people grow by one of the most innovative thinkers of our era. Read, learn, apply, and enjoy. God bless!

Ken Blanchard
San Diego, California
January 1998

FIRST WORDS

▼▼▼▼

THE JOURNEY TO THIS BOOK began in 1960 on a brilliant autumn day in Minnesota. I was thirty years old then, an ex-schoolteacher and a successful life insurance agent. I was successful enough that I had been asked by Federated Insurance of Owatonna, Minnesota, to create a course to train their agents. Although I had instantly answered yes, I had no idea at all what the course should be about. I only knew that I didn't want it to have anything to do with how selling and business were conducted at that time. Business was a low-trust, adversarial world then, and I was completely open to new ideas.

On that autumn day, I found myself wandering the University of Minnesota campus, with two of my kids tagging along. There was football in the air and the excitement of a university coming back to life after a sleepy Minnesota August.

We walked past the university bookstore. Outside, they were having a sidewalk sale, dumping books at a dollar each to make room for new inventory. Purely by accident, I picked up a book in the psychology section and opened it to an article titled, of all things, "The Hierarchy of Relative Prepotency," by Abraham Maslow. A grabber of a title. (And no, I had no idea what it meant.) But as I scanned it, I saw that Maslow was writing about human potential and what would become his famous pyramid of needs. Something inside me said this was important stuff. I bought the book, went home, read the article five times, and made a decision.

The next morning, I took a leap of faith and called Maslow at Brandeis University. I told him I was an insurance agent and asked if I could visit him for a day. Maslow being Maslow, he said, "Of course." Back then, Maslow was emerging as the third force in psychology—Freud being the first force and the behaviorist school the second. Maslow represented an island of humanism in a sea of behaviorists at most all universities. The humanists essentially rejected the behaviorists' claims that there was nothing to human psychology but behavior, nothing but "stimulus-response." The humanists knew there was more to us than just responding to stimuli; we weren't simply Pavlov's dogs.

Abraham Maslow was clearly the most outspoken and well respected thinker of the humanist school, so I was nervous when I arrived for our meeting. How much time could a man in his position have for a young insurance agent? But Dr. Maslow was open, kind, and gracious. We met for a whole day. I remember thinking all the while that he was treating me like a peer, instead like some salesman from the very distant (and obscure) Midwest. We talked about people and about his pyramid of needs. Because we were both fathers, we talked about our kids and raising children in the "wild sixties."

And then the conversation took a turn that affected the rest of my life. Maslow talked about Eupsychia. He used the term *eupsychia* to mean "the good mind," in much the same sense that *euphoria* means "the good feeling." Eupsychia was his imagined island of a thousand people who were all self-actualized. *Self-actualization* was his term for that relatively rare group of people who were motivated to discover their true selves and answer their deepest questions about meaning and purpose. Self-actualized people were those who had met their physical survival and status needs; they were now motivated to grow, to serve, and to reach their full potential.

Close to the end of our conversation, Maslow asked—I thought rhetorically—what I thought living on that island would be like. He leaned forward, pointed at me, and said, "Why don't you go find out?" Although I probably could not have articulated it this way at the moment, finding eupsychia—"the good mind"—and helping others discover it became my life's purpose.

A few years later—after having designed a very successful sales training course—I launched Wilson Learning Corporation. I almost named it Eupsychia—with Maslow's blessing—but I could not spell it and no one else could pronounce it. Our purpose statement became "helping others become as much as they can be." We became the second-largest training company in the country and based much of our work on Maslow's theories and fellow psychologist Carl Rogers' work in counseling.

In 1982, I sold Wilson Learning and launched Pecos River Learning in Santa Fe, New Mexico. It was another step in my journey to discover eupsychia. At Pecos River our focus was on helping individuals and organizations everywhere rediscover their courage and creativity and use them in the service of creating a better world. It has always been my purpose to help facilitate and accelerate the journey of individuals and organizations toward Maslow's vision of "the good mind." This book is in large part a result of what we have learned from helping well over 500,000 people and countless organizations on that journey.

In this work, we stand on the shoulders of giants like Abraham Maslow. These are the revolutionaries who have changed the way we think about ourselves, and their ideas are the themes that run through this book. To Abraham Maslow, Viktor Frankl, Albert Ellis, Kurt Hahn, and Maxie Maultsby—and others—we owe a great debt. They are the artists; we, the copyists.

After flunking retirement yet again, my latest endeavor has been to create an in-depth life curriculum that deepens the concepts found in this book. You can find out more about it at the website, Thegreatgameoflife.com

Larry Wilson

Notes from the Authors

THIS IS A COLLABORATIVE PRO-
ject. It represents the work,
sweat, tears and learning experience of the staff of Pecos
River and Larry Wilson and
Associates. Although every-
one contributed, there are two people
without whom this book would never
have been born. Linda Brown and Bill
Payne helped us launch the ideas, the
teachings, and the Pecos River organization. Linda has always been the
guiding light of Pecos River and playing to win. Her brilliance and passion
have illuminated our path for the last
ten years. The late and sorely missed
Bill Payne, to whom this book is dedicated, was the heart and soul of the difference we have tried to make in the

world. Beyond Linda and Bill there are the many others: Staff and clients who have helped this book grow. Loring Johnson, Leslie Stephen, and Kathy Bork, our editors. Ray Bard, our publisher, and Suzanne Pustejovsky, the book's art director. Tonya Murphy, who transcribed *endless* interviews. Dr. Vicki Stoddard, our friend and consulting psychologist. Dorothy McIntyre, of the Minnesota High School Athletic Association, for her help with women's sports. All the Pecos River trainers and clients whose mid-night voicemail messages kept us deep in ideas. To all we owe thanks.

So although this book is written in the voice of one person to make it easier to read, it is more truly the voice of many—the staff and clients of Pecos River who come to work every day to help individuals everywhere rediscover their courage and creativity and use them to create a better world.

Larry Wilson and Hersch Wilson
November 1997

It makes a difference whether we consider ourselves pawns in a game whose rules we call "reality" or as players in a game who know that the rules are "real" only to the extent that we have created or accepted them.

—Paul Watzlawick, Richard Fisch, and John N. Weakland, *Change*

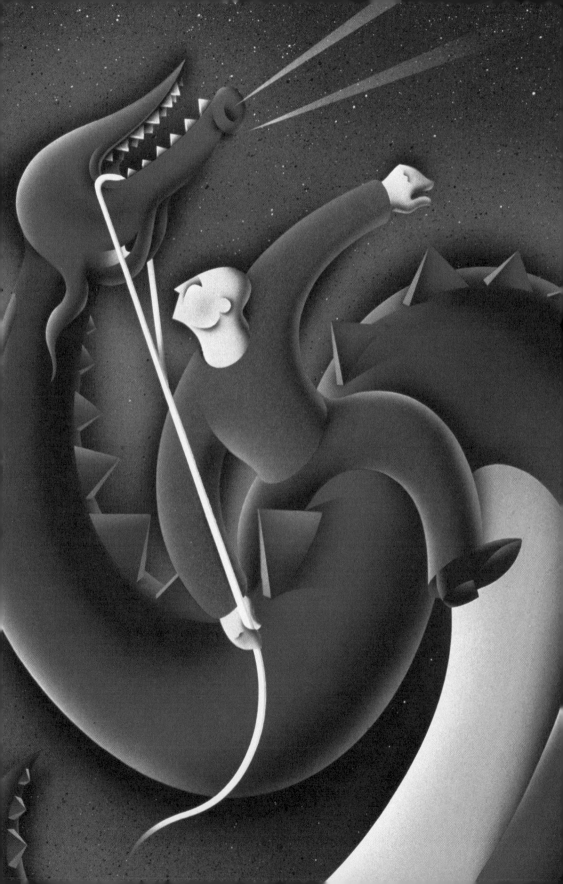

PART

I

▼ ▼ ▼

Adventure defined:
A difficult endeavor
in which the outcome is
unknown, but the possibility
of great reward exists.

The
Adventure

West of the Pecos River,

throughout the ranches of New Mexico and West Texas, cattle graze on ranges that are so large that it is not economical to hang gates everyplace a road crosses a fence. So ranchers invented the cattle guard—a ditch dug across the road with metal bars spaced every few inches to span the ditch at road level.

Cattle guards were a great invention. Cars and trucks could drive right over them, but cows couldn't walk through them. The cattle were effectively fenced in. Of course, there is one problem with cattle guards. When a pickup truck (the vehicle of choice in the West) runs over a cattle guard at fifty or sixty miles an hour, the jolt to the driver, passengers, cargo, and suspension is hellacious.

Once upon a time, some enterprising cowboys got together to tackle this problem. Figuring that cows were not terribly bright, the cowboys decided to fill in the ditches, and paint stripes across the road where the bars used to be to keep the cows from straying. It worked. Cows wandered up to the painted cattle guards and said to themselves, "Whoa! That's a cattle guard; I can't go any farther."

Painted cattle guards became the rage. The cows, being mostly an unchallenging lot, accepted the painted cattle guards, chose not to question their fate, and spent their days milling around grazing in their assigned pasture.

But, of course, no solution is perfect. A few years passed, and then, one day, a couple of cowboys found a herd that had crossed a painted cattle guard to graze in the rich, lush grass close by the Pecos River.

Here is what the cowboys concluded: One cow had gone up to the painted cattle guard and for the first time really examined it. She squinted her eyes and looked at it hard. Thoughtfully, cautiously, she put one hoof on

the cattle guard and discovered that it was just paint. "Paint!" she thought. "This isn't a real cattle guard! I have been fenced in all these years by a pretend cattle guard!" This went against herd wisdom. It was common knowledge that cattle guards were impassable barriers; it was the way things were!

But now this cow thought hard and long about the consequences of being fenced in by paint. And although she was terrified, she put another hoof

on the paint and still nothing happened! She took a deep breath and walked across. Then she led the entire herd across that painted cattle guard.

That is what we call a smart cow.

What made that smart cow successful wasn't necessarily extraordinary courage. She was successful because she took the time to examine the painted

> *Most people would rather die than think: many do.*
>
> —Bertrand Russell

stripes on the road and to think about them. She considered real evidence rather than relying on herd wisdom. Only then did she discover that the cattle guard— which had kept her fenced in for all those years—was just made up!

The moral of this admittedly tall tale is this: At first glance, most true adventures seem dangerous and full of barriers—like cattle guards that herd wisdom teaches us not to cross. But if we stop to examine what is fencing us in and then think about it, we often discover that the barriers are simply paint. If we can clearly understand the difference between what is real and what is paint, we can begin adventures we had never before imagined.

What you are about to read is a guide to the most important adventure that any of us will undertake—the adventure of our lives. The premise is simple: We have a choice. We can remain fenced in all our lives by herd wisdom and painted cattle guards, or we can choose to examine the cattle guards, break through, and go our own way.

To go our own way requires us to think clearly and deeply. To begin, put yourself in the place of a reader of the *London Times* in 1907. You're sitting in your comfortable den. You pick up the paper and an odd headline catches your eye:

**WANTED:
PEOPLE TO
UNDERTAKE
HAZARDOUS
JOURNEY**

THE ADVENTURE OF YOUR LIFE

Wanted: People to undertake hazardous journey—small wages, bitter cold, long months of complete darkness; constant danger; safe return doubtful; honor and recognition in case of success. This ad was placed by the explorer Sir Ernest Shackleton, who was looking for people to accompany him on his expedition to the South Pole. He was describing as honestly as he could an adventure, an endeavor in which the outcome was uncertain, where great reward was possible but only at the cost of risk, hard work, and danger.

> **S**ecurity is mostly a superstition. It does not exist in nature. Avoiding danger is no safer in the long run than outright exposure. Life is either a daring adventure or nothing.
>
> —Helen Keller

Whether he knew it or not, Shackleton's words were also an apt description of most people's lives.

Our lives are adventures. At work, at home, and in our communities, we undertake often-difficult endeavors in which the outcomes are unknown, where success and fulfillment are possible—not guaranteed—but only at the cost of working hard, taking risks, and sometimes even facing danger.

On any adventure we have a choice. We can try to simply survive it—clinging to the hope we will get to the end unscathed—or we can try to thrive, allowing the adventure to grow us in ways we could not have imagined when we began. Clearly, the objective of the adventure of our lives is not simply to survive ("Whew, I got to my death safely!!") but to thrive in it and grow.

Here is what we mean.

THRIVING

In the late seventies at Wilson Learning Corporation, we developed "Wellness," a program directed at helping individuals develop their physical, emotional, mental and spiritual selves. The intended outcome of "Wellness" was helping people become not only more successful but also more fulfilled. (Success and fulfillment are linked as a theme throughout this book. The self-actualized people Abraham Maslow wrote about were in the hunt for both.)

We looked at the question of wellness this way: When we get sick, we go to doctors. A good physician takes us—we would hope—from being sick to being "not sick." We often live our lives thinking that because we are not sick—not in pain or dysfunctional—we are well. But, in truth, we are more often simply "not sick."

sick ------------- *not sick* ------------- *thriving*

This distinction is easy to see with physical health. We have the flu, we go to the doctor, we are told to rest and drink lots of fluids, and eventually we get over the flu. We are no longer sick—but often we are nowhere near our optimum state of physical health. We aren't sick, but we still could be overweight, not getting enough sleep, not even remotely in shape . . . we aren't physically thriving.

Surviving versus thriving

There are lots of people who are simply not sick during the adventure of their lives: They are not happy at work; they are in the middle of their lives but have lost their sense of direction and purpose. Others aren't consistently feeling the way they want to feel. Some find themselves facing great opportunity—an adventure—but they find themselves unwilling to take the risk.

Many of us are just surviving our lives, thinking that we are doing what we're supposed to do. We think we're okay—but we're not truly thriving in our one and only great adventure.

What we want to explore in this book is how to thrive in the great adventure of our lives. We are also going to suggest that what is crucial to the endeavor is emotional, mental and spiritual growth.

GROWING UP EMOTIONALLY

Here is the paradox. Learning how to thrive requires much thought and reflection, yet the answers are not to be found only through intelligence. To use the poet's dichotomy, thriving involves not solely matters of the head, but also matters of the heart. The question of whether we'll thrive in our adventure or settle for less is directed primarily at our emotional intelligence. The people best able to thrive in the adventure of their lives are those who are emotionally mature.

> **EMOTIONAL MATURITY:**
>
> **We define emotional maturity as having access to and control over the emotional energies required to respond optimally to life's events.**

New York Times science writer Daniel Goleman summarizes emotional maturity in his best-selling *Emotional Intelligence* this way:

1. Being self-aware—*knowing our emotions, recognizing a feeling as it happens;*

2. Managing emotions—*handling and managing our feelings appropriately;*

3. Motivating ourselves—*marshaling emotions to pay attention, delay gratification, and stifle impulsiveness;*

4. Feeling empathy—*understanding others and recognizing their emotions;* and

5. Handling relationships—*building and maintaining relationships.*

When we are emotionally mature, we are much better able to solve the two categories of problems that cause much pain, dysfunction, and frustration (both personal and organizational). Intrapersonal problems (within ourselves) show up as lack of confidence, self-doubt, lack of clarity, anxiety, and fear. Interpersonal problems (between ourselves and others) result in conflict, lack of trust, ineffective communication, and, again, lack of clarity.

GROWING UP SPIRITUALLY

The handmaiden of emotional growth is spiritual growth. Let's go back to the idea of the adventure. An adventure is an endeavor in which the outcome is uncertain and contingent on many factors, some within our control but many not. And yet, our adventure is framed by this certainty: It is temporary. Our adventure is completed by our death. It is the great and looming presence of death that gives poignancy and urgency to our lives.

I was sixty-three years old and at the very top of my game. I was making a lot of money, well known in my field. I went for my annual checkup and the doctor said, in that analytical, medical way, "We need to do more tests, but we think you have bladder cancer." More tests, diagnosis confirmed.

Nothing we can do, no position we hold can protect us from the capriciousness of life. Now you're here, now you're not. I caught my cancer early enough to stop it from metastasizing for now. But the lesson is indelible. There was a time when we did not exist. After we die, there will be a time when we don't exist. In between is a brief second in time in which we exist. These truths apply to each of us.

Why am I here?
Given the "now you see me, now you don't" nature of our lives, the important questions become the spiritual ones—Who am I? Why am I here? What difference will I make? The spiritual adventure is to find and live the answers to those questions.

That death frames all this is not morbid to the emotionally and spiritually mature. It is simply the truth. It might be painful, we might choose to deny it for much of our lives, but "growing up" requires that we eventually embrace this truth. Our deaths can illuminate our path; they can create clarity. We can use the fact of our eventual death to inspire us to get on with it.

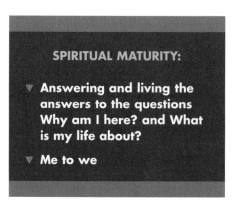

SPIRITUAL MATURITY:

▼ **Answering and living the answers to the questions Why am I here? and What is my life about?**

▼ **Me to we**

The large picture is not about "me"

Spiritual growth also requires moving from the position that "life is about me" to seeing ourselves as part of a whole, one thread in the tapestry. Fritz Kunkel, a German-born psychotherapist, calls this shift "me to we."

With this shift in perspective come many gifts. When we are involved with others, we are less fearful. When we serve others, we get feelings of fulfillment and joy that are difficult to dig out of the flinty ground of "life is about me."

LEARNING WHAT WE ALREADY KNOW

Growing up is an important theme of *Play to Win!* and the key to thriving in the adventure of our lives. When Plato wrote that learning is rediscovering what we already know, he probably wasn't talking about quantum physics. More likely, he was talking about the themes and ideas presented here. It seems common sense—we know that emotional maturity and spiritual growth are vital to any hope we have of becoming truly fulfilled and successful.

Yet it can't be said that this is common practice. It takes discipline and work to understand and control our emotions, to grow up emotionally. It takes courage to fully absorb the truth that we will die and then to use that truth to propel us toward our reason for being here. It often takes a wake-up call of crisis proportions to see that we are not the center of the universe, but rather, that we are here to help and serve others. Unfortunately, we often don't come to that understanding until it is nearly too late, until we are looking back on our lives wondering "What if . . . ?"

IF YOU COULD DO IT ALL OVER AGAIN . . .

Our friend and colleague Dick Leider's primary mission in life is helping people plan and live careers that are successful and meaningful. For his remarkable book *The Power of Purpose*, Dick interviewed hundreds of people in their seventies and eighties. (He initially interviewed two hundred couples in the late 1970s and has followed up with approximately thirty interviews every year thereafter.) He asked these simple questions: If you could live your life over again, what would you change? What is the wisdom that you would pass on? Although he got many different and specific responses, most fell into three categories.

I would see the big picture

Dick's subjects often said they were so busy living day to day that they missed truly living their lives—all of a sudden they were sixty-five. The only time they reflected on who they were and why they were here was in times of crisis. They wished they hadn't relied on crisis to inform their decision making and their life's direction. They wished they had taken more time to reflect on the big picture, including the spiritual aspect of their lives.

I would be more courageous

The second pattern Dick heard was the wish to have been more courageous, to have taken more risks, especially at work and in relationships. At work his subjects would have risked being more creative and finding work that was meaningful to them. In relationships, they would have focused on having the courage to be better friends, parents, sons, or daughters.

I would make a difference
They also wished they had understood earlier that the essence of living is to make a positive difference. No matter how successful or unsuccessful people were, they expressed a hunger to leave a legacy. Reflecting back, they wished they could have made more of a difference.

YOUR CHOICE

See the bigger picture, live more courageously, and make a difference. The point is to ask yourself right now, in the present, Do these themes pique my interest, touch my heart, stir my soul? Is that what I want my work and life—my great adventure—to be about? Or will I wait, change nothing, "survive" the adventure of my life, and look back and ask myself "What if . . . ?"

The choice, of course, is yours.

The map
If you choose to thrive, this book is a guide. It will make choosing to thrive in your adventure easier. Part II: Rethinking the Game is about redefining winning and success. Part III: Thinking Differently about Thinking covers different ways to understand how we think and how our thinking influences how we feel and how we act. In Part IV: Solving Problems and Creating Results, we will introduce the thinking tools that you can use every day to help control how you respond to the events that occur on any adventure. In Part V: Work and Life Strategies, we will examine what thriving in life and work really can mean. In Part VI: The Spiritual Adventure, we

will look at the elements of growing up spiritually. Finally, in Part VII: Choosing Growth, we'll walk you through a simple plan for helping you thrive in *your* adventure.

The journey

But *Play to Win!* is just a book. You cannot thrive in your life just by reading a book, no more than you can satisfy your appetite by reading a cookbook. Life is an adventure to be fully experienced, lived, experimented with, and committed to. A book is a poor substitute for experiencing what the adventure has to offer. But a good guidebook can help—it can provide tools to make the adventure easier and the insights of others to help illuminate your experience.

This book is such a guide. It is full of tools and perspectives that we—and many of our clients—have found useful in our adventures. The first perspectives that we want to discuss—and challenge— are the beliefs we hold with almost religious fervor about winning and losing, success and failure.

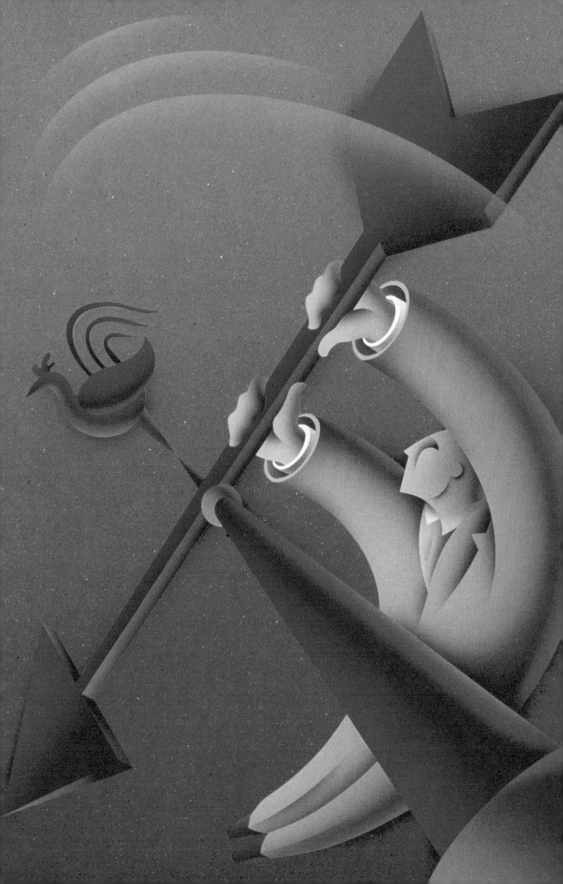

PART II

▼▼▼

Game defined: A set of rules specifying the goal of the game and the roles of the participants, including the permissible actions of, and information available to, each participant, the criteria for establishing progress, the criteria for termination of the game, and the distribution of payoffs. Finally, the rules specify why the game is being played.

Rethinking the Game

To a great extent,

our personal adventures are caught up in the games of Winning and Success. We work hard at winning and succeeding. We teach our children to be winners. Being a winner and being successful (or at the very least, appearing successful) are such important payoffs in our society that many of us are deeply involved in these games personally and professionally.

In this part of *Play to Win!* we want to challenge—gently—those beliefs. We want to redefine the very idea of winning and suggest that success as a payoff is not nearly enough.

REDEFINING WINNING AND LOSING

If life is an adventure and our task is to thrive, to grow in every aspect of our being, how do we win? Do we win by beating everyone else? By getting there first? By winning the most prizes?

When we are talking about playing to win in the adventure of our lives, the traditional definitions of winning and losing don't hold up. Of course, there may be times when we need to call on our competitive natures to accomplish what we set out to accomplish. But competing to defeat someone is only one way of responding to the events we encounter. In fact, in the great adventure of our lives, there is no one to defeat.

The first step in redefining winning and losing isn't determining whether you've defeated all comers or won all the prizes; it is more fundamental. The deeper question is: "On this adventure of your life, what is the game you're playing?"

> **W**hy is it that in order for somebody to win, other people have to lose? It doesn't always make sense in business, and it rarely works in relationships or in day-to-day life.
>
> —Wendy Steele, ORION Learning

We are going to consider two "games." The first—and more common—game we call Playing Not to Lose. The second and rarer game we call Playing to Win.

PLAYING NOT TO LOSE

Playing Not to Lose is ultimately about avoiding fear. Having said that, if you ask people if they experience fear in their personal or professional lives, they will most likely tell you no. Here is why. We are bright people, and most of us learned long ago to avoid situations in which fear (defined differently for each individual) might come up.

In many situations, this makes eminent sense. We avoid going down a dark alley because we might be confronted by muggers—or worse—and experience fear. We have a built-in early warning system that alerts us to these kinds of situations so that we can avoid them and thereby avoid experiencing fear. Unfortunately, this precognizant ability often leaks over into other areas of our lives where we aren't at true risk.

PLAYING NOT TO LOSE:

Avoiding situations where we might lose, fail, be emotionally hurt, or be rejected.

Avoiding situations where we believe we are at risk often starts early in life. A friend tells his version of an archetypal story.

He was in third grade. Like most third-graders he had a vivid imagination and lots of energy, and he loved to draw. One day in class, he was drawing away, oblivious to everything but the smell of crayons, the feel of them on the paper, and the wild and wonderful colors they produced.

All of a sudden, he noticed that the other kids were laughing at him and making fun of his drawing. It stung. The well-intentioned teacher admonished the other children for laughing, but reminded him that the assignment was to color inside the lines.

He felt deeply embarrassed and decided at that moment that he never wanted to experience that kind of embarrassment again. He made a simple decision never to draw again. Even though he enjoyed drawing, it became more important never to risk being "humiliated."

It's not important to know whether our friend wanted to be an artist and his aspirations were destroyed in third grade. We will never know—because he chose a path designed to avoid situations where he might be embarrassed like that again. His early warning system went on alert at that moment and it generalized. It no longer warned him simply about drawing; it helped him avoid situations where embarrassment might occur. It influenced all kinds of choices he made later in life.

Our early warning systems are put on full alert early in our lives to help us avoid situations in which our status or sense of belonging might be threatened. And so when we are asked whether we experience fear, the reasonable answer is no, because we have often spent a lifetime avoiding those situations where fear or embarrassment might result.

We call this strategy Playing Not to Lose. Playing not to lose is like playing tennis against eight-year-olds who have never played before. We are in no jeopardy of "losing"; we can declare ourselves winners after every match . . . but we are not playing (or living) anywhere near our potential because we are afraid of losing.

Playing for survival

We often play not to lose because we believe that the consequences of embarrassment, or "losing," are awful. "Awful," according to psychiatrist Dr. Maxie Maultsby (a man we will meet in the next part of this book) means "100 percent bad."

In our imaginations we believe that the consequences of being rejected are so awful that they are akin to psychological death—"I'll be embarrassed *to death*." When we play not to lose, the game is about survival. To survive we need to avoid the awful stuff that we have imagined over the years might happen to us if we take a risk.

This avoidance leads to the regret that Dick Leider's seniors were talking about. They chose not to take the risks required to grow in relationships or at work because they were afraid of what might happen. So you avoid telling people you love them because they might not say it back. Avoid striking out on your own because you might fail. You play it safe.

> **ASK YOURSELF:**
>
> ▼ How do you define winning? At work? With your family? In other aspects of your life?
>
> ▼ What situations do you avoid because at some level you think there is a risk of losing a sense of belonging or status?
>
> ▼ What situations do you avoid that could be important to your personal or professional growth?

PLAYING TO WIN

In its simplest sense, Playing to Win is consciously choosing to not automatically avoid situations in which we might fail, be embarrassed, or be rejected. Why on earth would we consciously choose to do something that could lead to failure, rejection, embarrassment, or worse? Because our goal is to grow. Playing to win is concerned with engaging with life, with the desire to thrive on the adventure. Emotional, spiritual, and intellectual growth are the game's payoff.

> *Courage is the price that life exacts for granting peace. The soul that knows it not knows no release from little things.*
>
> —Amelia Earhart

This is easy to see in the area of emotional growth (although easy to see doesn't mean easy to do!). Take a key component of emotional maturity: bouncing back from failure and rejection. There are no doubt some genetic aspects to the ability to "bounce back." Yet, even so, the way we are going to truly improve on our ability to bounce back is by experience—by trying something out, failing, getting over it ("I didn't die!"), trying again, and so on. Remember how you learned to ride a bike? The human being is wired to learn by experience. This is especially the case for emotional and spiritual growth.

Playing to win means consciously choosing to experience those situations that will help us grow. Further, it means going into those situations wholeheartedly, committed to going as far as we can with all that we have and learning from whatever happens.

PLAYING TO WIN:

Consciously choosing to go as far as I can with all that I have and learning from whatever happens.

ASK YOURSELF:

▼ Where have you chosen to take risks and, as a result, grown—often in ways you didn't expect? That's playing to win.

▼ Where have you given 100 percent regardless of the potential for failure—and been satisfied with the effort regardless of the outcome? That's playing to win.

A CONSCIOUS CHOICE

We choose to play not to lose because we believe our emotional survival is at stake. We choose to play to win in order to learn, grow, and thrive. Although it is not often that black and white, the critical moments of our lives and careers often come down to a choice between the two: Am I going to play to win or am I going to play not to lose?

Playing to win is about making choices—especially the important ones—consciously rather than simply letting our early warning system direct us away from possibly difficult situations. As we will see, consciously choosing requires us to know what we want, to understand how we want our lives or a particular decision to turn out. Consciously choosing requires us to think more clearly and objectively about how to get to the game's payoff. Being more conscious of our important choices also means that we are constantly asking ourselves: Are there real things here to fear (do I really need to fear embarrassment, for example), or am I just following the herd by balking at another painted cattle guard?

To be comfortable being uncomfortable

Playing to win also asks us to take on this ability: to be comfortable being uncomfortable. Often the desire to be comfortable is how the choice to play not to lose is made. I will be more comfortable if I don't take this risk. I will be more comfortable if I avoid asking difficult questions: Am I doing what I want to do? Do my life and work have meaning? Am I in denial? Am I in love or am I just passing the time with someone? Am I choosing comfort over growth?

Emotional and spiritual growth demand of us that we be uncomfortable, that we take risks when we are uncertain of the outcome. Playing to win asks us to be comfortable in that uncertainty. Playing to win asks us to be comfortable asking uncomfortable and difficult questions of our soul. This is a path to growth.

A while ago I had the opportunity to see this in practice. I was sitting with a senior executive team that had decided to embark on a significant change effort. They had all agreed intellectually to the need for the change. Now the launch moment was at hand. You could see that the emotional impact was just hitting them—we might fail, we might look ridiculous if we fail, and so on. The CEO spoke up first: "I am uncomfortable with going ahead." A chorus of executives joined him in expressing their hesitation. They were all emotionally uncomfortable with taking the risk of doing what they knew intellectually was for the best.

Finally—in what was an act of courage—a woman in the group stood up and spoke her mind. In essence she said, "This is between choosing to be comfortable and continuing to do the same old stuff—which might in the long term put us out of business. Or we can choose to do the right thing and as a result accept being uncomfortable. As leaders, it is our responsibility to not avoid doing what is right because we want to be comfortable."

There was an "uncomfortable silence," but her impassioned words

> **P**laying to win as a perspective liberates you. More frequently than not, it helps me be more challenged by the uncertainties and ambiguities of the world rather than just trying to avoid them. My confidence in terms of working through difficult issues has gone way up.
>
> —John Griffin, secretary of natural resources, State of Maryland

carried the moment. The group chose to go ahead. Playing to win asks us to choose being uncomfortable in order to grow.

WINNING

Winning, then, does not mean defeating someone else or achieving a goal that doesn't really stretch us. Winning in the adventure of our lives means that we are going as far as we can with all that we have and learning from the experience. Goals are good—they make interesting benchmarks. Competition can help us push ourselves (the word *competition* comes from the Latin word *competere*, which means "to strive together").

But are you really stretching yourself when you try simply to "win"? Are you growing? Are you pushing your limits? Do you feel alive? Do you feel excitement, the anxiety of trying something that really pushes your abilities, good exhaustion at the end of the day, an I-can't-wait-to-get-up-in-the-morning sense of anticipation for each new day? Are you going as far as you can with all that you have? Are you playing to win or are you playing not to lose?

▼   ▼   ▼

Clearly, playing to win is how we thrive in the adventure of life. Playing to win becomes an easier and more natural response when we are emotionally mature, when we have access to and control over the emotions needed to respond optimally to life.

Growing emotionally—the fundamental building block of playing to win—is the focus of the next two parts of this book.

RETHINKING SUCCESS

Being successful has traditionally been the payoff of any game; having the trappings of success is how you know you've won. And yet, as most of us know, simply being successful—even though we obsess over it—is only one dimension of what it is to be a human being.

A number of years ago I held a dinner for some of the top-performing second-year salespeople in the insurance industry. After an hour or so of shoptalk, I asked how they were feeling about their success. Silence. Then they all looked around the room at each other and a few of the more outspoken began to speak. They were terrified, they said—the more successful they became, the more pressure they felt to be even more successful. One of the salespeople said she felt like she was chasing a rabbit, but no matter how fast she ran, the rabbit kept getting farther and farther away. It made her feel desperate.

IF I'M SO SUCCESSFUL, WHY DO I FEEL SO BAD?

What was going on? These salespeople had discovered what they thought was the formula for success and they were off and running. But something had gone wrong. Why?

People claim they want to be successful because they'll have financial security and be able to buy the things they want. If you ask them, "Why do you want financial security?" or "What will you get if you buy the things you want?" they'll probably answer, "I will feel the way I want to feel," "I'll be happier, more emotionally secure," and so on.

What we really want, it seems, is happiness or emotional security. What we believe (and advertising reinforces this belief every waking minute of our lives) is that we can get that feeling by becoming successful. It is as if someone sat us down at the beginning of our careers and whispered the magic word: "Success." What we thought we heard was that life was about

> **P**eople think they are seeking success but what they really desire is fulfillment.
>
> —Dean Griffith, Griffith Laboratories

being successful above all else! If we were successful, we would get the feelings we were after—fulfillment, happiness, and emotional security.

But we misunderstood. Success is fine; making money is usually a good thing. But the truth that we all discover, sooner or later, is that there is no direct and automatic correlation between success and the feelings of joy, happiness, and emotional security we crave. Success rarely creates the feelings we want.

This was brought home to me by the late Dr. Viktor Frankl, the psychiatrist and author of *Man's Search for Meaning* who spent three years in Nazi concentration camps. In the late 1970s, Dr. Frankl and I shared the speaker's platform in Vienna, where we addressed the annual meeting of the International Young Presidents' Organization. When I spoke, I used slides, music, and props to get my points across. Not Dr. Frankl, who was seventy-six years old at the time. He addressed the group with simply a blackboard and chalk.

Frankl drew a line on the blackboard that he labeled "failure" on one end and "success" on the other. He said that much of our lives are spent working hard to be successful.

Failure

Success

Success is primarily defined by external measures—how much money you make, your rank in the company, and the respect accorded you by your peers. Being successful seemingly always involves being measured against others. As Walter Hailey, an old

Texas friend, used to quip about money, "After a certain amount it isn't the money; money's simply how you keep score." If you want to be seen as successful, you have to make a lot of money and collect a lot of trophies.

Frankl believed that there is a wholly separate dimension commonly left out of our thinking and planning, but one that is critical to the health and happiness of human beings. He drew a vertical line across the horizontal line and called it the depression-fulfillment line.

Fulfillment is the deeply felt sense that your life is full, whole, complete—that you have expanded to "fill up" your potential. Fulfillment is knowing that, if you died tomorrow, your life would have meant something, that it was going in the right direction and you were making a difference. Fulfillment, unlike success, is largely defined by internal measures, by how we feel about what we're doing or have done.

With the fulfillment-depression line in place, Frankl had created four quadrants. As we discussed the meaning of the diagram, it was easy to understand how people who saw themselves as a failure could be depressed, or even how people who were highly

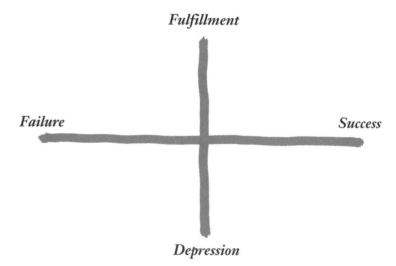

successful could feel depressed. What was difficult for this room full of highly successful individuals to understand was how someone could be a failure yet be fulfilled. To illustrate, Dr. Frankl read to the audience three letters. Each was filled with a deep sense of fulfillment and meaning. But the punchline was that the writers were all people on death row. These were individuals who were clearly on the far left of the failure-success line, and yet they had a tremendous sense of fulfillment.

This paradox was a true eye-opener for that room of "successful winners." Remember, everyone in the audience was working very hard in their companies, in part to acquire feelings of fulfillment and emotional security. And yet here they were, hearing about death row inmates who seemed to be more fulfilled than they—even though the prisoners were seen as outcasts.

The letters brought Frankl's simple point to life. Fulfillment is a separate dimension, not linked to whether we are successful.

> *I wouldn't care if I lost it all; I'd just start all over again, because I know I can do it. I'm not fearful of that. Even if I did have an economic collapse, I know that I can build something; I've done it before. . . . If I lost everything, it really wouldn't matter. I have personal happiness, I have personal security. The security is internal. It's not in my bank account.*
>
> —Helen Mills, Aon Consulting

Fulfillment comes from the drive to discover and live a sense of meaning, from answering the questions Who am I? Why am I here? The larger point he left us with was this: There are people all around us who are in pain. They are in pain because they are putting all their energy into being successful and they are not getting—as a reward—the feelings they want. They don't know what to do because they believe that the game is solely about success; they don't realize that success is only part of the equation.

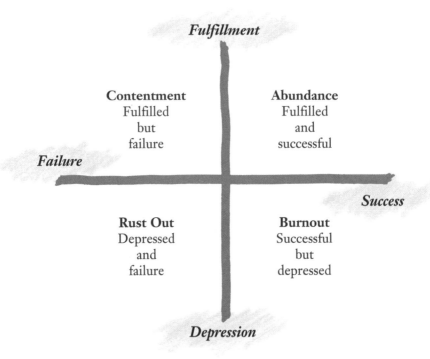

As a result, we think, "If I can just get this big deal, I'll feel different." And we do, temporarily. Then the feelings wear off and we are in the chase again. "I need another fix." "I need a promotion and more money." "I need to just work harder and then I will get what I want." It is a game that never ends and we cannot seem to "win."

BEYOND SUCCESS

You cannot find fulfillment by chasing success, by working harder, by running faster. You find it by stopping and thinking differently. By asking yourself what it is that you really want. What is your life really about? If you want to thrive, you have to pursue both success and fulfillment. They are separate dimensions; each requires time and energy. Achieving one doesn't necessarily mean you'll achieve the other.

We largely know what is required of us to be successful—hard work, perseverance, talent, and a little luck. We are less sure—as individuals and as a culture—of what is asked of us to be fulfilled. What must we do? How must we change to have those feelings?

Frankl wrote that fulfillment comes from three possibilities: the first is through creativity and meaningful work; the second is through relationships and love; the third is when confronted with unchangeable fate, to be able to change our attitude toward that fate—what he called turning suffering into human triumph.

> **S**uccess—everybody wants to be successful. Success by definition is accomplishing your objective. In other words, you've done what you have set out to do. Most people think that success makes you happy, but success and happiness are not necessarily related. The connection is this: if success is getting what you want, happiness is wanting what you have.
>
> —Billy Weisman, Weisman Enterprises, Inc.

▼ ▼ ▼

Meaningful work, significant relationships, and the ability to control your attitudes and feelings in the face of what life hands you—these form the path to fulfillment. It is a deeper and richer vein of living than simply taking the King Midas road to success, but it takes work and effort.

To begin, we need to rethink what winning and losing mean. Here is what we think of them: For the purposes of *Play to Win!* winning is going as far as you can and learning from whatever happens. Your goal is success and fulfillment. To play at this level, to thrive in the adventure, you often have to redefine your game and what your life and work are about. You start by working with the most powerful ability you have—the ability to think.

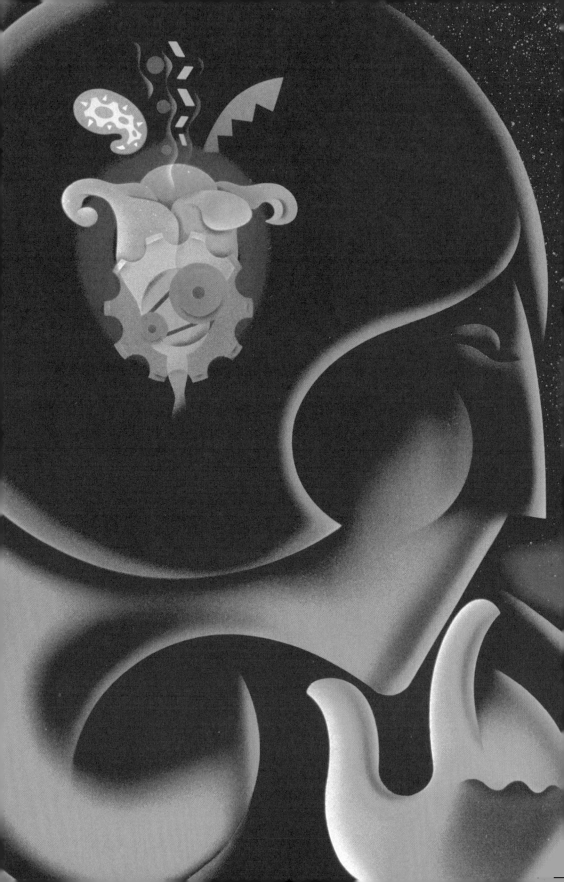

PART III

▼▼▼

People seldom think about what they think about. They think about how they feel. They think about what they do. But, what is causing what they feel and do is what they think about. Which they seldom think about. What do you think about that?

—Dr. Maxie Maultsby

Thinking Differently about Thinking

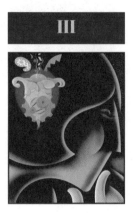

III

What often stops us

from going as far as we can is that we don't think clearly. If we are not thinking clearly, it is difficult to be good at the first two characteristics of emotional maturity: recognizing and controlling our emotions.

Our approach to thinking clearly grew out of a problem I was trying to solve with our Wellness Program in the late seventies, which was designed to help people thrive physically, emotionally, and spiritually. The problem wasn't that people didn't know what to do to change their lives for the better. That would have been easy to solve: just give them information. Individuals usually knew *what* to do—exercise, quit smoking, lose weight, relax more, and so on.

The problem was that for a variety of reasons—denial, comfort, fear—they simply didn't know *how* to change. And no change meant no growth. Helping people choose to change and then actually accomplish the change was the problem we had to solve, and we spent months trying to get to the root of it.

Out of the blue, I received a phone call from a dear friend, Walter Hailey, a down-to-his-boots wildly successful Texas businessman. Walter said, in his West Texas drawl, "Larry, I gotta tell you about a man that you have to meet." Walter's teenage son wasn't doing too well. Walter and his wife had tried all sorts of options when they heard about a psychiatrist in Lexington, Kentucky, Dr. Maxie Maultsby. They ended up sending their son to Maxie for three weeks. Walter's son came back a different person. Walter said he had another son who also wasn't doing so well, so he sent him too, and it was the same story. Finally, Walter said, "Hell, I wasn't doing all that well myself so I went down and spent a week with Dr. Maultsby, and he completely changed the way I think."

> *What we are talking about is a higher level of mental discipline. So often people go off in this search for more meaning, but they go in the wrong direction. They look for a guru who's going to tell them the answer. But that is not how it happens. What is really required is a process to think more clearly. It requires effort, focus, and energy on our parts. It isn't a quick thing and it isn't mystical—and that is an important message. Thinking more clearly is a very specific kind of mental discipline.*
>
> —John Allison, BB&T

Well, as you can imagine, I was one of Dr. Maultsby's next visitors. Since then, Maxie and I have become close collaborators and friends. We have worked together through two of my companies and through Maxie's transition from the University of Kentucky to the head of the Department of Psychiatry at Howard University Hospital.

Maxie started out in general practice in the fifties. After a few years of practice, he noticed that at least half of his patients had nothing medically wrong with them. As Maxie recalls, it mildly depressed him to realize that he wasn't helping these people feel better. As he reflected on these cases one by one, he realized the cause of the illness in many of them was anxiety and worry. The anxiety was caused by not being able to deal appropriately with events in their lives. They were the "worried well." They tended to worry themselves sick over problems that were either beyond their control or problems that were not that significant.

Maxie decided to go back to school and do a residency in psychiatry. Soon after, he discovered the leading-edge work of Albert Ellis. That discovery led Maxie to develop Rational Behavior Therapy (RBT). This was the fourth force in psychology, cognitive psychology (stimulus—think—respond). It became Maxie's intellectual home.

Maxie's work and the framework of cognitive psychology were based on the idea that much of the anxiety, anger, and worry we carry around is caused by irrational thinking. We can influence and most often control our feelings by examining and learning new ways to think. Maxie's legacy has been giving people the tools they need to better cope with the events in their lives that are causing the anxiety and the worry.

Maxie's approach—which we adopted and have taught since launching our Wellness Program in 1979—is that learning how to think more clearly and more rationally is how we are best able to understand and control our emotions, and thus how we can grow emotionally. In thinking more clearly, we become our own best coaches.

I CANNOT FAIL,
I CAN ONLY
LEARN AND GROW

Think about the way a good counselor—like a good friend—can help when we are in need of aid. She helps us sort through the jumble of feelings and conflicting thoughts to find the truth—as painful as the truth might be. She asks questions like "What are you feeling?" "Why do you feel that way?" "What are you thinking?" "What is causing you to act the way you act?" "What are you going to do differently to feel better?" She helps us challenge irrational reactions ("I'll die if I don't get this job!") and choose a more logical and beneficial way of thinking.

Most of the time—which is Maxie Maultsby's point—we are not our own best counselors. Instead, we tend to simply react to events—we worry, we get angry, we feel anxious or helpless. We don't think about why we feel the way we do. Stuff happens, we have an emotion, and we react.

THINKING ABOUT WHAT WE THINK ABOUT

Maxie's point is that to be our own best counselors, *we have to learn to think about what we think about.* Psychologists call this metacognition: getting out of the forest of our feelings and emotions and examining our thinking from 30,000 feet. Thinking about what we think about allows us to sort through what is rational and what is irrational and make better choices.

"THANKS FOR THE $25!"

Here is a practical example of what this means. This is the story of how self-coaching and thinking about what I think about changed my life by changing how I think about failure.

Now, at the time this story takes place, I had no idea who Maxie Maultsby was or that there was such a thing as cognitive psychology. Maxie was working with the "worried well," and I was one of them. I was desperately worried about failing, as an insurance agent and as a provider to my growing family. Failing—especially in business—is right up there with "losing" as one of the cultural "mortal sins."

Then I had an extraordinarily lucky learning experience. I was twenty-four years old, married, with three young children. We had recently moved from Sheldon, Iowa, where I taught high school history and drama, to the big city of Minneapolis, where I began to sell life insurance.

Three months into my new job I was miserable. I was—by my twenty-four-year-old reckoning—failing, a new and "awful" experience for me. We were living with my parents because we had no money, and we were going deeper into the hole every month.

I was making plans to get out of selling and find a new career. Then a friend, with the intention of helping me quit, sent me a book that changed my thinking about my situation. The book was *Man's Search for Meaning*, by Viktor Frankl, about his experiences in the Nazi concentration camps, how he survived and what he observed. His most salient observation was that we each have a choice—he called it our "final freedom"—in how we choose to respond to even the grimmest of circumstances. That is how he turned suffering into human triumph.

This book gave me this insight: I had a choice about how I was thinking and responding to what was happening to me. It became clear to me that I was choosing to wallow in depression—hoping to be rescued—instead of having the courage to stick with my career change.

I remember making two critical decisions. First, I decided to stay in the business and not run away. I decided that I would not allow any sale—made or lost—to determine who I was. This simple decision was a minor transformation in perspective for me.

The second decision came as a gift from my enlightened and thoughtful manager, Pug Lund, a former All-American football player from the University of Minnesota. Pug could have fired me and cut his losses, but instead he helped me rethink and reframe the experiences that I was having every day.

Each day I would make a call, be rejected, and go into an immediate tailspin. The tailspin caused me to think—irrationally—that I should never be rejected; being rejected was a sign of failure. Being a failure meant, of course, that I would soon be unloved and on the streets. Or so the thinking went that drove my anxiety. I took each rejection as a personal attack, which made it doubly difficult to go on the next call.

Pug helped do the math to help me better manage my thinking. At that time, like most rookies, I had to see about twenty prospects to make one sale. The average commission on the life insurance policy I was selling was $500. Pug taught me to divide the $500 by the twenty calls it took to produce a sale—$25. Thus every call on every prospect was worth $25.

Pug taught me this: I would make a call; I would be told "no"; and I would consciously force myself to think, "Thanks for the $25." Next call, another "no," another "Thanks for the $25." Whenever I did make a sale, I'd say the same thing to myself: "Thanks for the $25."

Those two simple changes—no one sale will determine my self-worth and "Thanks for the $25"—helped me change the way I interpreted what was happening to me. It took me a few months, but once the new thinking became internalized I felt less depressed and I also became more client-focused because I wasn't using all my energy to focus on "ain't it awful." Because my behavior changed and I became more persistent, my results began to change. After a

> **Y**ou should never be embarrassed or feel bad because an experiment failed. That's not failure. You carried out an experiment and it didn't work. It is not even failure if you carry out a whole series of experiments, come up with a theory, and then find out that there are ten exceptions to it. That's not failure. When you stop testing, stop trying things—that's when you fail, and that is when you should be embarrassed.
>
> —Eric Carlson in *Changing the Game*

while, it was taking me only ten calls to make larger average sales, and the average commission rose to $1,000. I could hardly wait to be told no and think, "Thanks for the $100."

> *I've learned that it is okay to be wrong. Making mistakes is the only way you learn. Decisions are not "you bet your life." If you are wrong, you're not immediately dismissed from your post and taken out and shot in the parking lot.*
>
> —Kathy Monthei in *Changing the Game*

The dramatic conclusion to this story is that those two changes in how I thought made me a very successful life insurance agent and I wound up as the youngest lifetime member of the prestigious life insurance Million Dollar Roundtable. I was asked to design a training program, which led to my conversation with Abraham Maslow, a career in speaking, Wilson Learning, and Pecos River Learning. My personal chronology of events starts with those two changes in how I chose to think about myself, about failure, and about persistence.

THINKING ABOUT FAILURE

Reframing the "failure" experience is one of the most dramatic examples of cognitive psychology at work, and it really comes down to thinking clearly and differently.

Since my insurance days, I have had more than just a professional interest in how people—especially successful people in high-risk businesses—think about failure. Over the years, I've collected lots of anecdotal evidence that points to the fact that many highly successful people have failed first, then had to reframe the experience of failing to see "failure" not as a negative but as a necessity—as the opportunity for significant and positive growth.

In 1986, we wrote about this phenomenon in a book called *Changing the Game: The New Way to Sell.* We looked at nine highly successful and ethical salespeople—five men and four women—who were all performing head and shoulders above their peers in what was a very difficult and highly competitive economy. We discovered that they shared a particular way of thinking about themselves and about work. We called this collection of abilities the Strategic Thinking Processes (STPs). They were the mental models that these nine people used—to greater or lesser extents—to frame their business lives.

The first STP—and the one particularly relevant to *Play to Win!*—is this: "I cannot fail, I can only learn and grow." At a very deep level, the people we looked at in *Changing the Game* took what others perceived to be "failure" experiences and turned them into growth experiences. More important, they really didn't believe in failure. They had taken the time and energy to get underneath that culturally powerful word and think about it, to ask, "What does failure really mean? What is the worst that could happen? Will I die? Will I be cast out into darkness?" What they discovered was that most of their fear of failure was based on—guess what?—irrational thinking.

THE STRATEGIC THINKING PROCESSES:

1. I cannot fail, I can only learn and grow.
2. My purpose is to help my customers get what they want.
3. Visioning: How do I want the future to turn out?
4. How can I create a long-term, mutually beneficial relationship?
5. How can I lead the team?
6. How can I add unexpected value to the relationship?
7. How can I leverage my learning?

Many of us, when we screw up, fail, or are rejected, do two things without thinking: first, we cover it up; second, we go right from the "failure" to "I'm worthless!" We take it personally and the learning we take away is to never, ever get caught in that kind of situation again. The lesson? Play not to lose.

The "game changers" came to the belief that the game was about learning. How they learned was by putting themselves at risk, "failing," learning, and then trying again. They were successful because they allowed themselves to make mistakes and to learn quickly from those mistakes.

▼   ▼   ▼

A completely different way of thinking about failure. Does this mean that our nine success stories weren't hurt by rejection or failure? Of course not. We are wired to be affected by perceived slights and insults. The difference is that these individuals had developed a process for thinking and dealing with failure that allowed them to bounce back faster, keep it in perspective, and move on. The core part of the process was thinking more deeply and clearly about what failure truly means— and what it doesn't. It is that kind of process that we want to explore next.

> **W**hat is the worst that can happen? . . . They can't bite you, they can't shoot you, they can't take your family hostage. All they can do is not have you work for them anymore. And then you can work for yourself or for someone else. Just make sure that you learn from what doesn't work. It would be a shame to keep making the same mistake over and over again.
>
> —Alan Braslow in *Changing the Game*

IT'S ALL
ABOUT RESULTS

Thinking clearly and deeply about anything begins with stopping and asking the big question: What are we trying to accomplish? Let's start with the idea that in work and life we are trying to do things that are intended to help us feel better (for example, avoiding unnecessary conflict usually helps us feel better) and to produce positive results.

THE RULES OF RESULTS

Results are external to us; they are a consequence of something we do. Think of results as what we accomplish—positive or negative—in life. A promotion is a result, being demoted is a result. Starting a business, finishing school, getting a speeding ticket, being in a healthy (or unhealthy) relationship with our children—all are examples of results. We have three rules about producing results.

Rule #1: You can't control the results you get

The results we get are out of our control; we cannot guarantee any result. This will come as a shock only to major control freaks, but the real world is full of outside influences, multiple variables, and random events. Try as we may, we cannot control anything external to us. Yet we often spend a lot of time and energy worrying about things—like the future—that are simply beyond our control.

The key word is *influence*. It's more accurate to say that we can many times (but not always) influence the results we get. *Influence* means that we can affect an outcome. We can shape; we can eliminate obstacles. By our actions, we can create higher or lower probabilities of getting what we want. For example, if we do the right things, we have a higher probability of get-

> **THE RULES OF RESULTS:**
>
> 1. We can't control the results we get.
>
> 2. The results we are getting are the results we should be getting.
>
> 3. If we want to change the results we are getting, we have to do something differently.

ting a promotion—but no guarantee. If we have dinner nightly with our children, we have a higher probability of creating a healthy relationship with them—but no guarantee.

Rule #2: The results you are getting are the results you should be getting

What kind of results *should* you be getting? No matter what you do, there is only one answer to that question: The results you *should* be getting are exactly the results you *are* getting.

For example, you're stuck in a dead-end job (a

> **I** remember once saying to one of my financial consultants—who used to worry all the time—here's what we're going to do. Today, we're really going to worry. For the first half hour of today, we're going to worry together. We're going to sit here and we're going to do nothing but worry. One half hour, uninterrupted worry. And then after that we're going to declare a moratorium on worry for the rest of the day. He just laughed and said you're nuts, you're crazy. But the point is, after that half hour, what will we have accomplished? If you're just going to sit and worry all day, it's not going to do you a darn bit of good.
>
> —Rob Knapp, Merrill Lynch

result). Well, technically you *should* be stuck in a dead-end job. Huh? To explain: In the question "What are the results you should be getting?" the key word, of course, is "should." A more scientific way of thinking of the word "should" is: "Anything that ever happened should have happened." What that means is this: Everything was there to make something happen; nothing was there to prevent something from happening; therefore, that which happened should have happened.

"Should" is not about predestination, fate, karma, the sins of the fathers, or voodoo. It is about the law of cause and effect. If you drop a pencil, it should fall to the floor if nothing is there to stop it

> *So many people spend so much energy on things that are beyond their control! It's human nature, but I constantly ask people anytime something comes up, "What do you have control over, what don't you have control over? What can you influence, or who can you go to that has some influence?"*
>
> —John Marshall, Dofasco Steel

from falling and if gravity is working to make it fall. Cause and effect. In the Buddhist's eye, we live in a lawful universe. If the pencil didn't fall to the floor, we would be dealing with magic.

Listen carefully the next time you watch an interview with a losing athlete or politician. He will often say, "We should have won!"

What he really means is *We could have won if we had done something differently*. We could have gotten different *results* if we had done something differently. And that leads to Rule #3.

Rule #3: If you want to change the results you are getting, you have to do something differently

No magic, no voodoo, no sacrificing goats—if we want to change the results we are getting, we have to do something differently. This is so simple, yet so misunderstood.

We often find ourselves wishing something were different but not doing anything substantially different to get different results. If you think about it, this is a little bit crazy. An apt definition of *crazy* is doing the same things over and over again and expecting different results. At a minimum this is an inefficient and ineffective way of thinking and responding.

Doing something different seems to be the key, which really means that we have to respond differently to the events—the positive, the negative, and the tragic—in our lives.

▼   ▼   ▼

To tie this all together, we can't control the results we get; results are external to us. We can only influence them. The results you are getting in your life are the results you should be getting in your life, because everything is there to create your results and nothing is there to prevent them from happening. So, if you want different results you have to do something differently.

> The adage that I have taken to heart is "If you always do what you've always done, you'll always get what you've always gotten." And you see that play out so much. People want change, but then no one wants to change the way they do business in order to effect a different outcome. It's amazing. It's palpable.
>
> —John Griffin, secretary of natural resources, State of Maryland

And therein lies the clue. To lay this out simply, what drives how we respond is how we feel. Emotions are the fuel of behavior. If we fear failure, we will avoid those situations that might cause it. When we feel anger, we attack. What greatly influences how we feel—whether we are afraid, angry, or jubilant—is how we think. To explain that, we need to talk about snakes.

THE SNAKE MADE ME DO IT!

Imagine three people in a room. Now imagine what each of these people thinks about snakes. Bill is from New York. He has never seen a snake, knows nothing about them. Emma is from the swamps of Georgia and has lived with snakes since she was a kid. She had them as pets, she now has a Ph.D. in herpetology, her license plate reads "SNAKE DOC." Then there is Henry, who had a bad experience with a snake as a kid. Henry is terrified of snakes.

For the purposes of our experiment, let's introduce a five-foot-long bull snake into the room. What happens? Henry is out the door; if there is no door, he'll make a door. Emma goes right for the snake and picks it up. Bill, our New Yorker, is curious—it is a large snake—but he is much more interested in lunch. And besides, even though Henry ran out of the room, Emma went right to the snake and picked it up. So Bill needs a lot more information to clue him in on how to react.

What caused these three different responses? The obvious answer is the snake. If the snake hadn't slithered into the room, no one would have responded. The snake in this illustration is really a metaphor for life. Whether we want it or not, life shows up—events happen.

Given that life is always showing up, given that the snake did slither into the room, what really caused the different reactions? The answer, of course, is not the snake, but each person's beliefs about snakes, their experience with snakes. Henry's history had taught him a sort of "See snake, feel afraid!" response and he ran. Emma had much more experience and history with snakes, including the training needed to tell dangerous snakes from ones that are safe to handle. Based on what her history had taught her, her response was to stick around. Bill had no history with snakes. The snake barely registered on his radar screen as an event—it was simply a novelty. He wasn't going to run, but he wasn't going to pick it up either. He was neutral.

What caused Henry, Bill, and Emma to respond wasn't SNAKE ———➤ RESPOND (the snake made me do it!). What caused their responses was SNAKE ———➤ "INTERPRETATIONS ABOUT WHAT SNAKES MEAN" ———➤ RESPOND (my interpretations about snakes made me do it). So, an event happens. We interpret the event and we

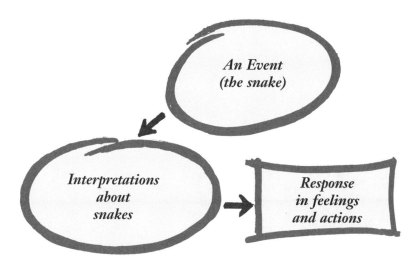

respond, based on our interpretations, with feelings and actions that influence the result we get.

A nonsnake example. It's Friday morning. You get a note from your boss that says, "I need to see you at 4:30 P.M." No explanation. The note is an event. You interpret the possible meanings based on the history of Friday afternoon "surprise" meetings in your company, what the "rumors" are, and so on. Without any further evidence, you end up thinking that it has to be bad news. All work now stops as you worry. You think about how your friend Sally was fired . . . right after a Friday afternoon meeting! You respond in feelings by being anxious and nervous. You walk into the meeting and, as a result of your interpretation of history, you respond in actions by sulking and being defensive. Of course, your boss notices all of this, which influences how she treats you (the result).

THE TRAGIC FLAW

In Shakespeare, every potentially heroic character has a tragic flaw. Othello has all the makings of a hero except for that jealousy thing with Desdemona. Hamlet is a king in the making, except he tends to brood too much.

We too carry around a tragic flaw in the way we think. Our tragic flaw is that we often believe that it is the snake—our boss, our spouse, our kids—that causes how we feel and how we act. "If it weren't for my boss and that stupid note, I wouldn't have gotten upset!" instead of "I got this note and I made myself upset!" We think that events directly cause feelings and therefore our responses. We see this clearly in children: "My sister made me do it." "The dog made me do it." "It's not my fault!" But we also see it to varying degrees in adults: "The note made me upset." "My boss drives me crazy." "I shook my kid because he wouldn't stop crying—it's his fault."

> *O**ur perception of an event or experience powerfully affects our emotional, behavioral and physiological responses to it. For example, if we are standing in line at the grocery store and think, "This will take awhile, I may just as well relax," we are likely to stay calm. . . . However, if we think, "This place is poorly managed. It is not fair to have such a long line," we may feel angry.***
>
> —Dennis Greenberger and Christine Padesky, *Mind over Mood*

When we think "The snake made me do it," two things happen. First, we are largely at the mercy of the snake—of the events in our lives—and we are simply victims. A snake shows up, we run, and we forever believe that all snakes are a threat. Second, we have no reason to stop and think that we might have caused our own response or that we have many other response options. We believe that the way we feel—depressed, angry, frustrated, bitter or happy, content or "in love"—is caused exclusively by the events of our lives. If good things happen, we're happy; if bad things happen, we're not; if tragic things happen, we don't know what to do. From this per-spective, there is no cause for introspection, for deeper thinking. The lesson learned is this: Seek pleasure and avoid pain. We are victims of whatever happens to us in life.

Certainly, good things, bad things, and tragic things happen to us. Life shows up. We cannot control events. What we can control, to a great extent, is what we think about those events, how we inter-pret what happens to us. By controlling our thinking, we can better manage our emotions and better control how we respond to the events of our lives. Remember: Emotions are the fuel of behavior.

HOW WE GET RESULTS

The Results Model is a graphic representation of how we get results. We've adapted this model from the work of Maxie Maultsby, Albert Ellis, and others in the field of cognitive psychol-ogy. An event happens, and our interpretations of the event rule how we respond. We respond with feelings and behavior. How we respond influences the results we get.

The bottom line
We cannot control the events that happen to us. Sometimes we can influence them, but life is far too capricious to be controlled. "Stuff happens." All we can truly control is our thinking, our feelings, and how we respond. If we want to change the results we are getting by responding differently, the crucial place to start is by controlling—challenging and changing—the way we think.

Changing results begins by coming to an important, and emo-tionally mature, realization: It isn't your boss, your kids, or your sit-uation that makes you upset. The truer statement is almost always, "Your interpretations of what your boss said or what your kid did made you upset." Instead of "You make me angry," the truer state-ment is "I make myself angry" (even though I may tend to make

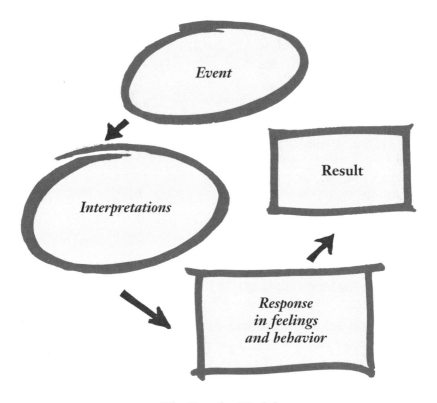

The Results Model

myself angry more often when I'm with you!). Our interpretations of the events of our lives—how we think about them—are what cause our responses. We are in control of our interpretations, our beliefs, and our thinking. That's the bottom line and that's the good news.

GROWING UP EMOTIONALLY

A huge step up in emotional maturity is taking responsibility for the way we think and the way we respond. Emotionally immature people tend always to blame the snake: "He did it, she did it, they did it, it did it to me." They do not take responsiblity for their anger, their worrying, or their lack of motivation. It is all those events that are causing them to feel and act the way they do. Emotionally immature people

> **T**he fundamental—simple but powerful—message about the Results Model is that whatever happens to us, we have a choice in the way we react. This is clearly true at work, and at home.
>
> —John Walker, Interface Europe Ltd.

tend to act as if they are not in control of their thinking, their feelings, or their responses. Growing up emotionally—handling and managing our feelings and our responses appropriately—begins by taking accountability for them. Emotionally mature people tend to understand that they can exert control over their feelings and responses by controlling their thinking. Emotionally mature people choose how to respond to whatever life hands them.

▼　▼　▼

Life will surround you with all sorts of events. What are you going to do about it? Will you be simply a victim of it all— swept away by the current—or will you choose how you want to respond? We can choose to be more emotionally mature by being accountable for our thinking. No more "The snake made me do it!"

We can best do this by making the humbling but truthful admission that our thinking, our beliefs, and our interpretations are normally—two important words—inaccurate and incomplete.

THE TRUTH DEFINED

The news was electrifying. Nothing like it had been seen in the history of treating autistic children. The process was called "facilitated communication" (F/C). The autistic child would communicate via a pointer on a Ouija board–like tool. Helping guide the child's movement was a trained facilitator, whose responsibility was to help move the pointer to the letter or to the number indicated by the movement of the child's hands.

All of a sudden these children who previously had been thought to be profoundly retarded were seen in a new light: as intelligent minds trapped inside bad bodies. Now these children were being mainstreamed, doing algebra, reading Shakespeare, writing poetry, all with the help of their facilitators and the tools of facilitated communication. It seemed to signal a profound shift in the way autistic children were treated.

One problem: Facilitated communication really didn't work quite the way people thought and believed it did.

Researchers were intrigued by the growing use of the process and alarmed by the increasing number of accusations of abuse leveled by autistic children using F/C. As a result they subjected the whole process to a number of experiments to discover whether the children were actually communicating through their facilitators (which was the prevailing and passionately held belief of proponents) or whether the facilitators themselves were unconsciously doing the communicating.

The results were devastating to the community of F/C facilitators and supporters. The research clearly and convincingly showed that the children were not communicating. In one series of 180 trials, there was *not one* demonstration of a child communicating. What the research demonstrated was that the facilitators were unconsciously doing most of the communication.

But how could this be?

INACCURATE AND INCOMPLETE

How could these bright, committed facilitators believe in something, see it as truth, when in the light of day, there seemed to be no objective evidence? Were they that wrongheaded?

The easy lesson is that the facilitators—with the best of intentions—simply got carried away in their passion to help. As a result, they made that simple but often profoundly tragic transition from wanting to believe that something is true to believing that it is true.

The more important lesson is that, just like those facilitators, almost every waking moment we hold beliefs and interpretations that are just as inaccurate and incomplete. These beliefs and interpretations control our feelings and control how we respond to events around us. If many of our beliefs and interpretations—especially those we hold about ourselves and others—could be subjected to rigorous experimentation, we too would probably be surprised to find out how incomplete and inaccurate our thinking is.

Yet the heart of emotional maturity is the willingness to subject our beliefs and interpretations to challenge and to change them in the light of new and more "objectively true" information.

> *The end of the road of self-awareness for me has been trying to make logical decisions based on the facts and to prevent lack of self-esteem from getting in the way of being able to deal with reality. . . . In our organization, the same thinking applies. We're going to look at the facts, we're not going to make things up because we wish they were so.*
>
> —John Allison, BB&T

TRUTHS AND BELIEFS

Admittedly, we are going into an area where wiser individuals have feared to tread—the tangled and emotionally charged area of beliefs. So it is important to frame exactly what we are going to address. Let's start by defining truth. (Not bad for a single chapter—it took Hegel an entire book!)

For the purposes of this chapter, we are going to define truth (not divine truth or revealed truth, but walking-around truth) this way: Truth is whatever you believe. Why? Because you wouldn't believe it if you didn't think it was true. Obviously there is more to truth than that, but in our minds—as we operate day to day—we make up what is true and then believe it all the time.

> **K**ids devise beliefs to explain anything. In their minds, they're trying to find a rational explanation. . . . A child is going to come up with a belief like, "If I hadn't jumped on the bed, then my grandma wouldn't have had a heart attack and died." Underneath that belief is the childlike belief that I am the center of the universe, I control and I am connected to everything that happens. Which is why I explain grandma's death as caused by me.
>
> —Tracy Burke, M.S.W

A lot of us are like kids when it comes to our beliefs—although we can be more subtle in practice. Our most deeply held "truths" don't necessarily, or automatically, line up with objective reality. But we act as if our "truth" *is* objective reality, and we will go to war to defend and protect our version of the truth, because it is what we believe.

We tend to think, talk, and act in absolutes. For example, I believe there is/isn't a God, or I believe/do not believe in a woman's right to an abortion or a fetus's right to live, and so on. We rarely examine our deepest beliefs; they are just what is "so," which leaves little room for a different interpretation. We get stuck in our beliefs often to the point of being struck blind and deaf to contrary "truths." And we tend to surround ourselves with people of similar beliefs; we don't naturally seek "belief diversity."

MAPPING THE TERRITORY

Let's introduce a less semantically loaded word than the words *belief* and *truth*. Let's use the word *map*. *Map* is a very useful label for our "walking-around beliefs." One function of a map is to guide us from point "A" to point "B." In a sense, maps explain the territory—this way will be rough going, this is an easier path. Our beliefs and assumptions function in the same way, as guides to help get us through specific situations or through life.

It's important to understand that the map is not the territory. When we look at a map we don't think, This is exactly what the territory looks like, down to the finest, smallest, nitty-grittiest detail. We know that most maps—by definition—are incomplete and inaccurate.

It's also important to remember that, in the early years of seafaring, mapmakers—using rumors and conjecture—simply made up what they thought lay beyond the reach of explorers ("A friend of mine was told by this other sailor that the captain said that there were dragons out there!"). Modern cartographers—with modern tools—spend much time and energy making their maps as accurate and detailed as possible.

Our mental maps are more often like the ancient seafarers' maps—inaccurate and incomplete. This doesn't mean they're always unhelpful. They're based primarily on our experiences and on what we've been told by the people we trust. As a result, our mental maps usually are good enough to help us navigate through work and life unless we wander way off into uncharted emotional or cultural waters. Our maps are usually good enough to explain how life seems to work.

But there are a lot of gray areas. Our maps are inaccurate and incomplete enough (like those of the F/C facilitators) that we continually get into trouble. For example, if we deeply believe that getting along, not making waves, and being accepted are important above all else, then we are very likely to be using a map that tells us

the safest route is "I need to be accepted and I fear being rejected."
When we respond using that map, we will seek acceptance as one of
our highest human needs. This inaccurate and incomplete map will
be an obstacle to thinking and acting independently if that would
jeopardize your status in a group.

▼   ▼   ▼

It isn't that "I need to be accepted above all else" is wrong; it
simply isn't accurately aligned with reality. We rarely need to
be accepted by a group in order to survive (as we will explore later).

Think of it this way: The maps of emotionally healthy people
are closer to reality; less emotionally healthy people's maps are farther from reality. Of course, it is never that black and white. Very
few of our maps accurately portray reality down to the smallest
details. In that sense, we are all a little less emotionally healthy than
we could be. Our mental maps of our territory are more like those
of the ancient mapmakers—some facts and a lot of conjecture.

From our perspective at Pecos River, a primary cause of emotional "dis-ease" in the workplace and in our homes is that we carry
around inaccurate and incomplete maps and we rarely do the rigorous "research" necessary to check them out and keep them aligned
with reality. We don't spend lots of time and energy trying to get
an accurate and complete picture of the terrain *before* we make
decisions.

You
Graduated
From MSU

Why are our maps inaccurate and incomplete? Because we make them up. In our classes at Pecos River we tell everyone that they are already graduates of "MSU," the

We all manage our daily lives, our important relationships and our emotional upheavals by means of the stories we tell ourselves about ourselves. . . . We all constantly elaborate narrative structures to explain and guide our behavior. Some of the material is historical truth, and some of it pure fiction. And some of it may just be made up on the spot to suit the need of the current script.

—J. Allan Hobson, *The Chemistry of Conscious States*

University of Making Stuff Up, and they graduated very early. We were child prodigies in MSU. You don't have to be a neurobiologist or psychiatrist to understand this. Making stuff up is our daily experience.

Imagine that it's a steamy 6:00 P.M., you're driving home from work, stuck in traffic, already fuming because you're going to be late for dinner. You've been trapped at a light for five minutes and your air conditioner is on the blink. In your rearview mirror, you see a car on the shoulder weaving in and out of traffic, horn honking. You think—your temper rising—"*What is this?*"

Soon the car is behind you, right on your bumper, horn blaring. You blow up. (And, not having attended the Pecos River "urban driving survival school," you aren't aware that the first rules are don't get out of your car and don't make eye contact.) You get out of your car and storm back to give this jerk a piece of your mind. What you find is a middle-aged man, pale and obviously frightened. He rolls down his window and he's crying; he can barely speak. He says to you, "They just took my kid to the hospital. She was hit by a car—she's in a coma. I have to get there. Please help me!"

Immediately you have a new interpretation of the event, a new map. You first believed (you made up) that the guy was a jerk; you then discovered (you received more accurate and complete information) that he was just like you, with a crisis that you could empathize with. You tell him to follow you; you jump in your car and lead the way to the hospital (*your* horn blaring).

Given very little information—blaring horn and erratic driving—most of us would quickly make up a narrative, complete with a cause (the guy's a jerk). We would go from a speck of information to making up an entire explanation, often the wrong story, the wrong explanation (that is, inaccurate and incomplete). As a result, we would respond inaccurately.

IT'S HOW THE BRAIN WORKS!

Making stuff up is not good or bad; it's how the brain works, it's how perception works. The brain is designed to quickly make stuff up that is good enough to help us survive.

We interpret reality, generalize, prejudge, and create meaning. As events come over the transom, we rapidly ask ourselves, "What is it? What does it mean? What should I do? Is it dangerous?" We can be wrong on one or all of the answers, but that rarely causes us to pause. We are constantly making up meaning and maps to help us muddle through our problems and lives as best we can. We do it down to the level of biology and physics. Light streams through the eyes, exciting electrons that the brain assembles and interprets (makes up) as a sunrise, a sunset, your husband or wife, a friend.

> *T*he primary billet of the mental system is not self-understanding, self-analysis or reason, but adaptation to the world, to get nourishment and safety, to reproduce and so pass on descendants. . . . It works to gain a quick fix on reality and guide action.
>
> —Robert E. Ornstein, *The Evolution of Consciousness*

DRIBBLE TWICE AND PASS THE BALL

Organizations of people—our families, communities, work teams, and companies—also make stuff up. We create a powerful map together and call it the "truth." Just like individuals' maps, the maps of human organizations tend to be inaccurate, incomplete, and often irrational.

A powerful example—because it was once so commonly held—is "girls" basketball. I have four daughters, all of whom are athletic and all of whom felt the effects of what happens when we collectively make stuff up.

Go back to 1970. "Girls" basketball was very different then, and very different from the game the boys played. If you were to go to a 1970s high school girls' game, the first difference you would notice would be that the players dribbled the ball only twice and then passed. The girl who caught the pass dribbled twice and then passed, and so on and so on. It made for a very stilted and slow game.

Why was this so? Let's imagine for a moment that everyone had the best of intentions; they wanted nothing but health, growth, and success for those kids. But somewhere, somehow, well-intentioned experts—dealing from existing cultural assumptions and traditional beliefs—made up that girls were incapable of playing physically demanding sports.

Since the beliefs and concerns coincided with the prevailing (made-up) beliefs about females at the time, they went largely unquestioned . . . it was common knowledge.

The rule became don't run down the court—it's bad for you— just dribble twice and pass the ball. The high school girls playing basketball, in general, never questioned the rules because their coaches and their parents, with good intentions, said this was what they could and could not do.

Looking back on it, in the age of full-court, physical women's basketball, it seems pretty silly and, of course, sad. It was sad if you were one of those girls doomed to play a game that limited your potential. It was sad if, as one of those girls, you simply assumed the mental map of your elders: "I am limited because I am a girl. I can only dribble twice and then I have to pass the ball."

But where was the evidence? Where was the research? Where was the critical thinking? Unless the physiology of women has changed dramatically in the last few decades, the logical conclusion is that all those rules were made up. It was a well-intended conspiracy of making stuff up, and it limited the thinking and the abilities of generations of women and men (who also made up that women couldn't play full-court basketball).

We make stuff up, it becomes what is true (our maps), and we respond out of those maps. The fatal flaw is that we rarely stop and ask, Is this really so? What is the evidence for my beliefs?

> **W**e have learned to challenge our beliefs all the time . . . we are rooted in thinking this way. We always take the devil's advocate position with each other, in a constructive way. We are always asking what are we making up and what is really so. We really have a lot of discussion around what our maps are. This has helped us stay grounded in reality and move the organization much faster.
>
> —Gordon Whitener, Interface Americas, Inc.

MAKING STUFF UP AT WORK

Of course, we are most at risk when we are surrounded by people who think the same way we do—who think, along with us, "*Of course*, girls can't play 'real' basketball."

In the organization, this dynamic operates daily. We make stuff up about the company, the customer, the competition, the workers, the managers, and ourselves, and we are surrounded by people who

WHAT YOU MAKE UP IS WHAT YOU GET

James O'Toole, professor of management at the University of Southern California, studied General Motors' leaders in the 1970s. He attended their meetings, interviewed managers, and researched the company. As a result of his extensive work, he developed a list of operating assumptions, the underlying (made-up) maps shared by GM senior managers in the 1970s:

▼ Managers should be developed only from the inside.

▼ GM is in the business of making money, not cars.

▼ Success comes not from technological leadership but from having the resources to quickly adopt innovations successfully introduced by others.

▼ Cars are primarily status symbols. Styling is therefore more important than quality to buyers who are, after all, going to trade up every other year.

▼ The U.S. car market is isolated from the rest of the world. Foreign competition will never gain more than 15 percent of the domestic market.

▼ Energy will always be cheap and abundant.

▼ Workers do not have an important impact on production or product quality.

▼ The consumer movement doesn't represent the concerns of a significant portion of the U.S. public.

▼ The government is the enemy. It must be fought tooth and nail every step of the way.

▼ Strict, centralized financial controls are the secret of good administration.

do the same thing. In most companies, not only do we not seek belief diversity, but we tend to hire and promote people who think like us. Especially as managers, we rarely surround ourselves with people who vociferously disagree—in the search for "truth"—with our opinions. Or if our subordinates do disagree, they are rarely given permission to wholeheartedly disagree. The net result is that in many organizations management rarely examines and challenges its deeply held and shared maps.

The Results Model applies to organizations as clearly as it does to individuals. In our organizations, our collectively held and made-up maps—whether they are close to reality or not—drive the responses that produce the results the organization gets (just as they did in the GM of the 1970s).

OUR LIVES ARE AT STAKE

Learning that we make stuff up can be an uncomfortable discovery, especially if we have clung to our maps at work or in life as unquestioned truth and we will listen to no other interpretations. The idea that, to a large extent, we make up our beliefs strikes at a

> **I**nspect every piece of pseudo-science and you will find a security blanket, a thumb to suck, a skirt to hold. What have we to offer in exchange? Uncertainty! Insecurity!
>
> —Isaac Asimov

very human desire to have certainty, to have absolutes, to be able to say this is true and this is not.

But the heart of the human experience—especially when dealing with ourselves and with others—is subjectivity, interpretation, and best guesses. Maturity is largely the willingness to accept a certain amount of subjectivity and uncertainty, to accept completely

> *Every judgment in science stands at the edge of error, and is personal. Science is a tribute to what we can know even though we are fallible. In the end the words were said by Oliver Cromwell: "I beseech you, in the bowels of Christ, think it possible you may be mistaken."*
>
> —Jacob Bronowski

different interpretations—different maps—of the world from those we cling to.

Maturity, just like good science, is in large part the willingness to let go of long-held maps—maps that were made up in the first place—in the light of more accurate and complete information. We need always to ask, Where is the evidence? What are other interpretations? What am I making up that is not based on reality?

IS IT ALL MADE UP?

You might be thinking that as writers we are suggesting that the gist of the "making stuff up" argument is that there are no deep or fundamental truths or knowledge—that it is all made up. But we are by no stretch of the imagination capable enough or arrogant enough to think that. The "larger picture" seems to be vast, unknown, and possibly inexplicable. Simply remember the birth of your children! The human experience is full of faith and wondrous things.

Where it seems vital to us to apply the principles of the Results Model is in day-to-day life—in helping solve those two classes of problems that plague us: what we make up about others (interpersonal problems) and what we make up about ourselves (intrapersonal problems).

DID YOU MAKE IT ALL UP?

Think about your life. Hold for a minute the hypothesis—as difficult as this might be—that the beliefs you hold about yourself and your place in the world are made up.

Your beliefs about yourself are inaccurate and incomplete. They are not wrong, not right—they are just maps. And many of these maps—which you made up from events that happened when you were a kid—are still running your life. You may have surrounded yourself with painted cattle guards: The time you were picked last for a team. The time you got an "F" in algebra. The time your dad—because he was really upset—called you stupid. The time your boyfriend dumped you. The time that teacher told you that you were really good—or really bad—in science.

We have created meaning—inaccurate and incomplete—out of these and a million other events in our lives. We don't think about them anymore; we don't hold them up to the light and think, "Gee, what did I make up about not being picked to play?" They simply operate unchallenged. We made them up and we operate twenty, thirty years later along roads that our deeply held maps set: I can't play. I don't get math. I'm stupid.

▼   ▼   ▼

In *The Road Less Traveled* Scott Peck writes that "mental health is the ongoing process of dedication to reality at all costs." One of the most important processes of our lives is getting to the reality of who we are, letting go of long-held maps—maps that were made up in the first place—and dedicating ourselves to answering those two questions: Who am I? Why am I here?

More about these questions in Part VI. For now, we need to follow the thread of being dedicated to reality—stopping to challenge what we have made up and making choices based on reality.

PART IV

▼▼▼

Solving Problems and Creating Results

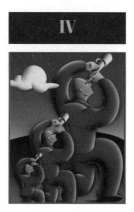

A troubled individual

seeking truth and enlightenment climbs the mountain to seek answers from a very wise old woman. When he arrives at her hut, the wizened old woman says, before our friend can even speak, "Ha! You have a problem, my son!"

Startled, the man asks how the woman knows he has a problem.

The woman replies, "Because you have eighty-three problems."

"How do you know that?" the man asks, somewhat indignantly.

As she sips her tea through a sugar cube, the old woman replies, "The universe is very fair: everyone always has eighty-three problems."

The man ponders this for a moment and then asks, "What am I to do with these problems?"

"Solve them!" the woman snaps.

"What will happen then?"

"Then you'll receive more problems, because everyone will always have eighty-three problems."

Then she adds, "There is only one other problem and that is the eighty-fourth."

"What's that?" the man asks in exasperation.

The old woman finishes triumphantly, "The eighty-fourth problem is believing that you shouldn't have eighty-three problems."

That eighty-fourth problem is a big one for many people. We think that we "shouldn't" have problems. But it seems quite apparent that having problems and solving them is what work and life are about. We no sooner solve one than we are rewarded with another, until the end of our lives, when either we have no more problems or we take on a whole new class of them. Who knows?

So, rather than complain and worry that we have problems, it seems much more productive to simply get very good at solving them. Day to day, we get the

> *L*ife is full of trouble, death isn't.
>
> —Zorba the Greek

results we want in life by solving life's problems effectively and efficiently—one after another.

This part of *Play to Win!* is about solving problems, about getting down to the daily work of living. It is about our ability to deal daily with our eighty-three problems and the events that really define what our life is about. It is through solving problems that we grow intellectually, emotionally, and spiritually. The bigger the problems we solve, the more we grow.

STOP, CHALLENGE, AND CHOOSE!

One of the treats of being a grand-father is watching my grandkids play soccer. While their parents worry about how their kids are doing, I can just enjoy watching them play and grow. One practice I watched was the first of the season for seven-year-olds. The coach was a young woman who clearly loved coaching those kids. That day—these were brand-new soccer players—the lesson was simply, Don't use your hands. In response to the "event" of the ball being kicked at them, the new players had to learn that they could use any part of their body except their hands to stop the ball. This was very "counterintuitive" and awkward for the kids. Amidst lots of laughter and giggling, the coach would kick the ball and the kids would have to think hard and quickly not to use their hands. They would say aloud to themselves and their teammates, "Don't use your hands!" There were lots of mistakes, but the kids took them in stride and were focusing on learning this new skill.

Flash forward three months. I went to one of the last games of the season. In this game, the same kids were automatically using their bodies to block the ball and avoiding "handballs" at all costs. They had gone through the process of learning, moved from awkward to natural. They had trained their brains, learned new responses to the "event" of the soccer ball coming at them that ultimately led to physiological changes in the brain.

RETRAINING OUR BRAINS

To help us get the results we want by solving problems more effectively, we often have to retrain our brains in precisely the same way. For us to learn the potentially new skill of responding with more control to the events of our lives, we have to go through the phases of learning and practicing a new process so it becomes automatic. The process is called Stop, Challenge, and Choose.

In essence, the process is this. Think about the Results Model. Instead of just reacting to an event (Here comes the ball. Throw up your hands!), we need to learn to stop, think about how we are interpreting the event (This is soccer, not baseball!), and then choose a response that is more effective (Keep your hands down and use your head!).

More specifically, Stop, Challenge, and Choose is used when we are confronted with an event or problem that initially makes us feel different from positive or neutral. The process is first to stop—to intervene in our thinking (we will explain how to do that in the next chapter). The next step is to challenge our maps and our interpretations of the event—what are we making up that is inaccurate and incomplete and not based on objective reality? What are other interpretations that are more objectively based that would help us respond in a more optimal fashion? Finally, the process asks us to choose to respond—to try out that new response.

WINNING BACK THE PLANT

A real-world illustration of the Stop, Challenge, and Choose process is a story told by Wendy Steele, now a partner, executive coach, and author with ORION Learning in San Diego. The problem was winning back the loyalty of employees. The event was an attempt by a union to organize a Coca-Cola bottling plant. The story you are about to read is not about unions being villains—the union officials were appropriately responding to what they saw as a need of the plant employees. Rather, this is a story of a company receiving a wake-up call about how employees felt they were being treated and how the company chose to deal with it by thinking differently about the problem.

This was a pivotal event in my career. It was 1994 and I was vice president of human resources for Coca-Cola Enterprises for the Florida region.

When we received the news from the National Labor Relations Board that the union had enough support from our workers to have an official vote on unionizing one of our plants, it was a very emotional event. The managers and supervisors in the plant immediately felt betrayed. "How could they do this?" "Why didn't they come to us first?" and so on. There was a lot of "us versus them" thinking. Because this was happening in South Florida, there were people with strong maps about strikes and unions. We had people who had been on both sides of the Eastern Airlines strike, where there had been violence on the picket line, and our situation could evoke a very emotional trigger-type response.

From that kind of thinking—us versus them—the natural response would be conflict with the workers, which would, of course, lead to more conflict, bad communication, and the plant's being unionized.

So we had to change the thinking—the map, if you will—about what it meant to be in this situation and how to regain the loyalty of the employees.

What I did, quite frankly, at the very first meeting with the supervisors—probably thirty front-line supervisors and managers at the plant—was have everyone stop and think about the situation we were in.

I said, "I'm going to take you on a little journey six weeks forward from this date, and I want you to envision the following." And I painted the scene: "We are all in a conference room down in the operations center inside the plant, and standing in front of us is a National Labor Relations Board officer who is counting the secret ballots one by one. This is the crucial point in time where everything that we have done in the six weeks prior has either convinced an employee that we're on the same team or that we're not.

"The feeling you will have as the vote is being counted is that your palms will be sweaty, your heart racing, and you will realize that

the balance of your future, how you're able to talk to your employees, the way that you want to communicate with them openly and honestly, everything hangs in the balance according to how that vote goes."

And, of course, when I looked around the room, I saw that their faces were ashen. It was a very emotional moment. It stopped them—and opened them up to seeing the larger situation.

Next, we had to challenge the rampant "us versus the employees" maps. Were there other possible interpretations than that of the employees betraying Coke and management?

I said, "Here is another interpretation. There are many, many reasons why union campaigns happen, but they are usually for very basic human principles. They happen because people—even our people—do not feel that they are being treated with respect or dignity. We have to realize that this is not about fighting our people; it is about treating them right so they that feel that they can trust us."

And I said that from this point forward we're going to let go of the anger and upset and instead focus on what created the problem in the first place, and then we're going to create a plan to go forward, because that's the only way we're going to get a positive result. Further, we couldn't allow ourselves to think or believe that the best outcome was "we win and employees lose." We had to work toward the idea that a win for us was a win for our employees. They had to be confident that they could work with management going forward. They would be voting for a future together.

With these interpretations in mind, we knew that if we were truly going to be successful we had to choose to respond differently than we had in the past.

So the first thing we did was tell our people that we hadn't been listening as closely as we should have, but we would now. We admitted that we had made mistakes. That started the open dialogue and discussion.

We committed to responding to all the issues. We created an open-door policy with the plant manager to let that happen. And we made it very easy for people to communicate. Some of our people did not speak English as well as others, and Spanish-speaking people were not getting all the information. So we designated a person who would conduct meetings in Spanish and English. From that point forward, any written communications went out in English and Spanish, which was the first time that had ever happened in Coca-Cola history. We also used videotapes that portrayed actual Coca-Cola situations on video to use as icebreakers to open up the communication. It was a concerted, six-week effort, right up to the final twenty-four hours, to change everyone's maps about what we could do if we worked together.

I think that, for the first time, our supervisors got a sense of the communication and commitment to employees that they were missing. They were so busy in their daily patterns that they forgot they were working with people who had personal problems, families, fears, and dreams.

When we had the election, the scene that I had portrayed for those supervisors was very accurate. The ballot counter was standing up there and I was standing next to the table, with a union person on the other side. The anxiety level was very high. When the final vote was counted, the woman from the NLRB looked at me, and then she looked at the union official and said, "Do you agree to this count?" and he said yes and I said yes.

The result was a two-to-one vote against the union. At that point, the place erupted, everybody jumped up out of their chairs. There were employees there, there were supervisors, there were four people from the union. The people were screaming and cheering "Yes!" It was like a scene out of a movie, and I thought, "Wow, that was what it was all about! If we worked together we could solve anything."

Analyze what Wendy and the supervisory group accomplished. The managers and supervisors were confronted with a problem that made them feel quite negative. They were headed for conflict with the very group they needed to influence, their employees. Wendy got them to stop—to step back and see the larger situation and pull back from the brink of conflict. Once that was done, she helped them challenge their interpretations of the situation. She then helped them see interpretations other than "we've been betrayed." After those critical steps were taken, it became easier to see, and thus choose, other responses and to work toward a positive result.

▼ ▼ ▼

"S top" is the step of intervening before we respond to an event without thinking. "Challenge" is the step of asking questions: What am I making up that is not based in objective reality? What are other interpretations of this event? "Choose" is the step of selecting a more appropriate interpretation and acting on it. Doing something different in order to influence getting a different result.

For many people, learning this process is very much akin to those soccer players learning not to use their hands—they had to retrain their brains to respond differently. It takes practice, making mistakes, lots of coaching, and trying again. But eventually it becomes how you think, and then—even if your world seems to be like an emergency room on a Friday night—you can stay calm and continue to solve your eighty-three problems.

THE TWO-MINUTE DRILL

" I was working the evening shift on a Friday night in the emergency department," Dr. Jamie Gagan, of St. Vincent's Hospital, Santa Fe, New Mexico, told us.

It was packed, there were only three nurses, and everybody was involved in trying to resuscitate a trauma patient to get him to surgery.

I had to stop, take a breath, stand back, and see the big picture. I had to think, "Wait a minute, we have more than one patient here, we have twenty patients. I need to know who is in the waiting room and make sure nobody out there is dying. I need to take the larger view of things, eliminate the life-threatening problems. Is there anybody here seriously ill that I don't know about?"

You have to stop and focus on the serious problems, get the life-threatening stuff out of the way, and then you can look at the other situations that are just problems.

What Dr. Gagan is describing is the underlying mental discipline of triage—the ability to step back, to get out of the frame of immediate activity, and see the larger picture. Once you can see the larger picture, then you can begin to do the work of triage—sorting big problems from the relatively unimportant ones and then solving the important ones first with the right resources.

LEARNING THE DRILL

For us to get the results we want day to day, Stop, Challenge, and Choose provides a similar mental discipline. The objective is twofold. First, it will help you stay focused on responding in ways that will produce the results you want in your life. Second, it will help you stay calm and engage the emotions that are most appropriate to the situation and to solving the specific problem.

We think of the Stop, Challenge, and Choose process as our "two-minute drill." It's a way of going from feeling an emotion that is different from positive or neutral, to managing it, feeling better, and responding more appropriately in two minutes (plus or minus a few minutes, depending on your experience and the significance of the event). Eventually, this process can become so automatic that it can happen as fast as you can think it.

> **W**hen a crisis occurs, I get very, very calm.
>
> —Tom Cigarran, American HealthCorp

EMOTIONAL CLUES

The first clue that you may need to use Stop, Challenge, and Choose is any emotion you feel that is not positive or neutral. Most of the time, feelings aren't negative, wrong, or inappropriate—they are how we feel based on how we think. Feelings are feelings. You need to become sensitive to your feelings, most especially when you are not feeling the way you want to feel—that's the time to use Stop, Challenge, and Choose.

Sometimes an emotion just sneaks up on you. You just feel upset or think, "Something made me depressed." Using this process requires you to get underneath and try to discover what thinking—what are you making up—that is causing your feeling. Granted, the problem could also be low blood sugar, brain chemistry that is a little out of whack, or inherited depressive tendencies, but in this book we are on the track of that powerful thinking sequence: EVENT ⟶ MAPS ⟶ RESPONSE in feelings and in behaviors.

EMOTIONAL CUES:

▼ How intense is the feeling?

▼ How frequently do you feel this way?

▼ How long does the feeling last?

Two points about the critical ability of identifying how you feel. (Remember that Daniel Goleman lists self-awareness—knowing our emotions—as a key component of emotional intelligence.) First, it's important to recognize the full range of human feelings. Try to accurately pinpoint how you're feeling. Analyze the feeling further—how intense is it, how frequently do you feel this way, and how long does the feeling usually last?

Second, remember that feelings and emotions are most often described by one word. If it takes more than one or two words, you are probably describing a thought. "I felt as if I wanted to tear his head off" is a thought—the underlying feeling is probably anger. Get to the feeling, not the explanation of the feeling.

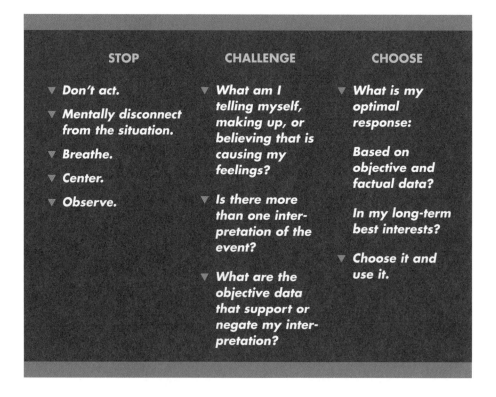

STOP	CHALLENGE	CHOOSE
▼ **Don't act.**	▼ **What am I telling myself, making up, or believing that is causing my feelings?**	▼ **What is my optimal response:**
▼ **Mentally disconnect from the situation.**		**Based on objective and factual data?**
▼ **Breathe.**		
▼ **Center.**	▼ **Is there more than one interpretation of the event?**	**In my long-term best interests?**
▼ **Observe.**		▼ **Choose it and use it.**
	▼ **What are the objective data that support or negate my interpretation?**	

STOP!

- *Don't act or react.*
- *Breathe.*
- *Center.*
- *Observe:*
    What is the big picture?
    Have I felt this way before?
    What does this situation remind me of?
    How was I feeling right before the event?
    (I was tired, I was happy, I was already
    upset, I was not paying attention.)

A fundamental premise: Anytime we intervene in our thinking to calm down and react more consciously, it's usually a good idea. Getting to calm is often the most important part of this process.

This doesn't mean that we can't or "shouldn't" feel joy, passion, laughter, or even anger. At issue is the fact that anger, worry, and fear along with other strong, "negative" emotions, while often vital and important, often block our ability to think clearly. Thinking clearly is a prerequisite to solving problems.

"Stop" helps us get to calm.

> **"S**top" really is the step of bringing to awareness your thinking and feelings. You can't challenge your thinking until you know what you're thinking. So a major part of "stop" is both the physical awareness and calming and pausing to ask yourself questions: What am I saying to myself? Have I felt this way before? What does this situation remind me of?
>
> —Tracy Burke, M.S.W.

BREATHE DEEPLY:

One popular breathing technique uses five heartbeats (for the sake of ease, think five seconds) to pace the breathing. Breathe in for five heartbeats, hold for five, and slowly exhale. When we breathe deeply, the chest expands to more than twice its size, allowing twice as much oxygen to reach the lungs. By holding for five heartbeats with the lungs fully expanded, we greatly increase the amount of oxygen that crosses into the blood stream.

Breathe

The first step in getting to calm is to work on it from the outside in—to intervene physiologically. The quickest way to do this is to focus on taking a couple of deep breaths—just like your mom told you to do before you got angry and "lost your head." It is more difficult to escalate into panic or upset when we are consciously trying to relax and we are breathing slowly and deeply. If you can, disconnect physically from the situation, from the event or the stimulus that is provoking you. If you feel anger, rage, or even anxiety rising, walk away for a few minutes and focus on getting yourself physically in control—calm and relaxed.

Center

More physiology. Check your posture. Are you scrunched up, waiting to be attacked? Are you coiling there ready to strike out in anger? Breathe, physically try to relax, unclench whatever you have clenched, stand or sit up straight. Focus on relaxing. In the martial arts they teach you to center, to put your body in a position that indicates being in control. So, stand up straight, knees slightly bent, and put your focus on your center of gravity—just beneath your navel. This is the balanced and centered stance.

Observe

We need to be aware of what is going on, just as Dr. Gagan made it a point to do. We need to step back and see the whole picture, take ourselves out of the action and be the observer. What is really going on that is influencing your feeling(s)? Why are you getting upset? What was the event? When exactly did you begin to notice that you were more depressed than usual? What was happening? Who was involved? What were you doing?

CHALLENGE

> • *What am I telling myself, making up, or believing that is causing my feelings?*
> • *Is there more than one interpretation of the event?*
> • *What are the objective data that support or negate my interpretation?*

When we are calm, the next step is to check out our thinking. What are we thinking about? How are we interpreting the event?

In the two-minute drill, we use three simple questions to help us challenge our thinking. Remember that *challenge* means simply to hold up the mirror and think about what you're thinking about.

*E*very time I think of something as an opinion, I say to myself, "Okay, that's my perspective. What's my perspective on my perspective?"

—Bob Root, ORION Learning

What am I telling myself, making up, or believing that is causing my feelings?

What is really going on versus what am I making up? Am I making up an interpretation that is not based on facts? For example, the Coke plant supervisors jumped immediately to "the workers are betraying us" without stopping to consider alternative interpretations. Their original interpretation (which was inaccurate and incomplete) was causing their feelings of anger and betrayal.

What are the objective data that support or negate my interpretation?

Look for evidence; look for what is objectively true rather than what you are making up. We will come back to this in the next chapter.

Is there more than one interpretation of the event?

Again, we will come back to this question in the next chapter, but the key skill is to look for interpretations other than the one that is making you feel "negative." Look for interpretations that might be closer to objective reality. For example, Wendy convinced the supervisors that another interpretation was that the workers might feel that they were not being treated appropriately.

CHOOSE

> • *What is my optimal response:*
>   *Based on objective and factual data?*
>   *In my long-term best interests?*
> • *Choose it and use it.*

First ask what the optimal response is—based on objective reality and in your best interests. The next step is to use it—to put into action new and more appropriate responses. For example, the Coca-Cola plant managers clearly came to understand that there were different interpretations from the ones they held initially. They also understood that it was in their long-term best interests not to be in conflict with their employees. Choosing these new interpretations allowed them to create responses that solved their problem and got the results they wanted.

FAKE IT UNTIL YOU MAKE IT

Learning to Stop, Challenge, and Choose doesn't mean that the process will instantly feel natural and easy! It was no doubt awkward and even artificial at first for those Coca-Cola plant supervisors to think about and act differently toward their employees, to be open and admit mistakes when at some level they still felt "betrayed." It is much like trying not to use your hands as the ball comes whizzing at you if you're a new seven-year-old soccer player. When we are learning something brand new, we have to deal with the fact that it feels phony—not natural. But if we stick with it—like those seven-year-olds—it will eventually feel more natural. Growth usually starts with the willingness to be comfortable being uncomfortable.

It is really helpful to write the process down, to see it in black and white, and then step away from it for a couple of days, and then come back and reread it and reflect on it and write some more. If it's a big issue, it's not something that I can resolve in fifteen minutes. It may take a week or a month. You know, it's kind of like peeling the onion a layer at a time until you really get to the core of the issue.

—Tim Flanagan, Mass Mutual

STICK TO THE PROCESS!

Stop, Challenge, and Choose is a process that is well grounded in cognitive psychology and—more important—is highly effective. Just the physical act of stopping and breathing—disconnecting from a tense situation before we respond in anger—allows us to see more interpretations and more options than we normally do.

It takes discipline, for the process often flies against that upwelling feeling to react, that product of the more primitive parts of our brain that know only fight or flight. But learning to Stop, Challenge, and Choose even in the most dire circumstances can give you a more productive way to think and respond in your world—you'll be calmer, see more options, respond in the ways that you want to respond.

In the beginning it may help to write down the answers to the Stop, Challenge, and Choose questions. Practice them in writing—ten or more times. Then the process will become automatic—a problem will be thrown at you and you will automatically Stop, Challenge, and Choose.

COMMON PRACTICE

Emergency room physicians have a common practice—a process—they use every time they see a patient. It's called the ABC's.

> *First patient. Does this person have an open Airway? Is she Breathing? Does she have Circulation? 53rd patient: Does this person have an open Airway? Is he Breathing? Does he have Circulation? 4823rd patient: Does this person have an open Airway? Is she Breathing? Does she have Circulation?*

You get the point. Different emergencies, same process—over and over again. They've trained their brains to solve problems with this process. Like a doctor in the emergency room, we can train our brains and commit to using the same process as our eighty-three problems in life come at us. Boss calls you into her office—Stop and breathe, Challenge what you are making up, and Choose a response based on objective reality and in your best interests. Associate loses your report—Stop, Challenge, and Choose. You get stuck in traffic on the way to a meeting—Stop, Challenge, and Choose. Your twelve-year-old son brings home a bad report card—Stop, Challenge, and Choose. Need to make a significant career decision? Stop, Challenge, and Choose. Should you take this risk or play it safe? Stop, Challenge, and Choose. Boss calls you in to her office for the hundredth time—Stop, Challenge, and Choose for the hundredth time.

▼ ▼ ▼

The primary purpose of Stop (What is happening?), Challenge (How am I interpreting what is happening?), and Choose (How do I want it to turn out?)—whether it is used for a brief moment or to deal with our larger and more complex problems—is to keep us from simply reacting to events. At the heart of the process is our willingness and courage to challenge our thinking—including the thinking, interpretations, and ways of responding that we have held for a lifetime. But it is that willingness to examine and challenge any thought or belief—to hold it up to the light—that is a fundamental aspect of growing up. Using Stop, Challenge, and Choose is how we work at becoming more emotionally mature—better able to manage our emotions and motivate ourselves appropriately—and thus more able to influence the results we want in life.

"A Little Thing Happens and the Drama Unfolds"

Challenge: To call into question that which we made up in the first place.

Recently, an "event" happened that turned my world upside down. My wife and I were selling our home, relocating, and were supposed to move in a little over a week. We had applied for a preapproved loan to buy another house so that we could get settled in as soon as possible.

One afternoon while I was on the road, I received a call from our lender advising me that a federal tax lien had showed up on my credit report. I didn't understand. I owed federal taxes as a result of a loss nine years ago but had been meeting my obligations for payment.

I called my wife to try and determine what had caused this problem. During our conversation we discovered that one payment had been misplaced and was not made on time. I was furious. I don't often experience this emotion and I pride myself on staying in control—but I lost it this time.

I started to "catastrophize" and make stuff up: Where are we going to live? Will we be able to even buy a house? We'll lose all our equity! We won't be able to retire! Why bother even living that long! My wife might as well leave me now and find someone else who isn't a bum. I'm going to die!

After the call and the "panic" session, I stopped and thought about what had just occurred—I was not at all happy with how I was responding.

I stopped. I literally lay down on my bed, focused on breathing and getting back under control. I thought through what had just occurred and challenged what I was making up that was irrational. This helped calm me down.

The next morning I called my wife and apologized, and we started talking about options and choices. I was able to think again. We came up with three solutions to our dilemma. It turned out to be a beautiful day.

That is the version of "A little thing happens and the drama unfolds" told by Dan Dean, formerly of the Aon Corporation. Most of us have been there. We think like Dan—"This the worst thing that could have happened"—and that influences how we feel and how we respond. When this happens, it is often because we are not challenging what we are making up.

THINKING RATIONALLY

The ability to challenge our maps—and that emotional cascade that Dan Dean experienced—is really about thinking and living rationally. The problem with the word *rational* is that it connotes someone who is unfeeling, who makes decisions based only on the facts, who doesn't understand intuitive leaps, great passion, or faith. Of course, none of that is true.

For the purposes of Stop, Challenge, and Choose, we are going to define rational thinking very specifically as using maps or interpretations that are based on objective reality and maps or interpretations held that are in our best interests. (Best interests doesn't mean selfish interests.)

This willingness to discover objective reality is fundamental to challenging all the obviously inaccurate and the subtly inaccurate stuff we make up that causes us to feel bad and act dysfunctionally.

For extra credit, define objective reality

Objective reality, as you no doubt recall from Philosophy 101, is a tricky and slippery idea. The argument can be made (as was no doubt made a number of times at parties during your sophomore

> **H**onesty to us is simply being consistent with reality. Integrity means that we're going to develop our principles logically based on the facts and to consistently act on those principles.
>
> —John Allison, BB&T

year of college) that there is no such thing as objective reality. Reality is all made up.

Hmmm, what to do? Here is our simple-minded test of objective reality: *Objective reality is what a camera would see.* To illustrate what this means, we do this little exercise in our classes: The facilitator picks a volunteer (usually of the opposite sex to increase everyone's awareness of the interaction). The instructions to the volunteer are to simply walk by the facilitator and say "hello." The facilitator's assignment is to walk past the volunteer with head down and not respond.

End of exercise.

And now the interpretation begins (the drama unfolds). When asked what they saw, routinely, people will say, "She [the facilitator] was really rude." "She insulted him [the volunteer]." "She is not a very caring person."

People "make up" that the facilitator insulted the volunteer because she walked by with her head down. But what a camera would have seen is just one person walking by another and saying "hello" and one walking past in the other direction with her head down and not responding. The camera sees "objective reality." Everything else is interpretation—stuff we make up. And there is a variety of different interpretations to that event—the facilitator could have just lost her best friend, she could be having a bad day.

Other examples. A camera would see you being fired; everything else that you are convinced is "true" at that moment is interpretation (you make it up). Being fired doesn't necessarily mean that they hate you or that you are an idiot or that you will never find another job—those are interpretations. However, we typically go right from the event of being fired to "This means I'm worthless." No, it doesn't! That is just an interpretation—inaccurate and incomplete. A camera would see you getting a promotion. Your belief that it means you are finally vindicated—or that now you are really in trouble

> **DISCOVER OBJECTIVE REALITY:**
>
> Discriminate between what a camera would see and your interpretation of what's happening.

because you are not worthy of the promotion—is just an inaccurate and incomplete interpretation. A camera would see you receiving that Friday afternoon note from your boss. As soon as you begin to think, "This means . . . ," you are making stuff up.

The first discipline: Discover the objective reality

We can't help but make stuff up—it is what the brain is designed to do. An important tenet of thinking rationally is understanding that we are mad meaning-makers, and that the meaning we pile on any event is interpretation. As a result, it is usually inaccurate and incomplete. Simply having the discipline to search for what is objectively true, especially when we are upset, will help us think more clearly, see more options, and not get locked into one way of thinking.

The second discipline: Diversify your interpretations

As we age—if we are not consciously keeping our minds in shape with this kind of discipline—our minds become a set of often unshakable interpretations

> **R**esults equal power. Better decisions create better results. Better options create better decisions. Diversity creates better options. Therefore, diversity equals power.
>
> —Jim Kearns, DuPont Fibers

DIVERSIFY YOUR INTERPRETATIONS:

▼ **What are other interpretations of the event?**

▼ **What are the interpretations of the event from people who think differently than you do?**

▼ **What are the interpretations of the event from people who are different from you in terms of gender, age, social status, nationality, or beliefs?**

---

of life and reality. Our thinking calcifies. We think, "This is how life is." "What my friends, associates, and the people like me think is the way things are."

It is the unwillingness to look beyond our noses, to ask for and see other interpretations, that is at the root of much prejudice and pain. It often is simply intellectual laziness. There are almost always other interpretations than ours. There is almost always an entirely different view of reality than ours.

The second discipline we need to learn—if we are committed to making choices based on objective reality—is to seek a diversity of other interpretations.

The third discipline: Determine what's in your best interests

There are times when it is very difficult to get to objective reality, especially when it concerns the soap opera of human interactions—he said, she said, they all said, and so on.

The third key premise of rational thinking is to hold maps that are in our best interests. Maxie Maultsby uses four questions to help us discern whether we are thinking with our best interests in mind.

To illustrate how this works, a colleague told this story:

James (not his real name) is the father of what he describes as a high-spirited and assertive ten-year-old daughter. Sarah is completely comfortable challenging authority (his) and she frequently loses her temper.

In the face of this, James found that he had an almost uncontrollable temper. He could feel the rage escalate in him if Sarah didn't do what she was told or if she talked back. There were moments when James was terrified by his desire to hit her. During one argument, when he lost control and jumped toward his daughter, she jumped back and he saw fear in her eyes. It was traumatic for him to realize that he was making his daughter—whom he loved more than his own life—fear him.

James stopped and thought about what was happening. He wrote it down. He was scaring everyone in the house with his temper (including himself) and he was putting his long-term relationship with his family in jeopardy.

DETERMINE WHAT'S IN YOUR BEST INTERESTS:

▼ Is my thinking helping me protect my life and health?

▼ Will my thinking help me achieve my short- and long-term goals?

▼ Will my thinking best help me avoid my most undesirable conflicts with others?

▼ Will my thinking help me feel emotionally the way I want to feel?

James decided, with the help of his wife, that what was in his best self-interest was a long-term, trusting relationship with his daughter—that was his priority. They could discipline, punish, or ground Sarah (forever came up as an option), but losing his temper would eventually cost him that relationship.

His plan—which he wrote down—was to, when he felt anger rising, first stop, disconnect from the situation, which often meant leaving the room until he got himself under control. Next, he would ask himself what he really wanted. Did he want to blow up, feel awful, and scare Sarah? Was that in anyone's best interests? This was his way of challenging his irrational thinking. Finally, he chose to relax, calm down, and focus on the vision of how he wanted each specific situation to turn out—with Sarah being disciplined but without his losing his temper. That vision helped him control his temper.

The way James was initially thinking violated three of the four principles of Maxie's questions. It was not going to help him achieve his long-term goal, a healthy and trusting relationship with his daughter. His thinking was causing undesirable conflicts with his daughter (and everyone else in their home) and making him feel miserable.

▼   ▼   ▼

We must ask these questions, over and over again, to help us think more rationally: What is objective reality here? What is in my best interests to believe? Learning to constantly ask these questions—especially in situations that are important—can make a significant difference in how we respond to problems and opportunities, events, and relationships. It is a thinking discipline that can help us live more rationally. And when we are thinking rationally we are much more likely to get the results we want.

CHAPTER 12

THE END OF LIFE AS WE KNOW IT

"It's a catastrophe!" "This always happens to me!" "I can't do it!" "It's impossible!" "That guy is a jerk!" "It will be *awful* if . . ."

Sound familiar? These are phrases that have run through our brains millions of times—sometimes so often that we believe them! When we talk about our maps being inaccurate and incomplete, it is most obvious both in what we call our "self-talk"—our internal narrative—and in what we say to others.

PARENTS SAY THE DARNDEST THINGS

Think about it this way. If you're a parent, you most likely would never use language like this to your child: "You *can't* do anything!" "This *always* happens to you!" "You're *awful*, you *should* be smarter!" "You *need* to be successful or you'll die!" We know that if we use that kind of language constantly with our kids— impressionable learners that they are—they may internalize all those messages and begin making stuff up about themselves: "I *can't* do anything!" "Bad things *always* happen to me!" "I'm *awful!*" "I *should* be smarter . . . "

Yet this is often the kind of language that runs unchecked and unchallenged through our minds as we think about ourselves and talk with others. The problem is that the brain (for illustration purposes only) is sort of a perfect stupid servant. It will give us anything we want. If we say, "This is the worst thing that ever happened—I'm miserable," we will feel miserable. Our brain won't say, "Wait a minute! Didn't we try misery last week?"

IRRATIONAL THINKING, INACCURATE LANGUAGE

From our experience and the research of Dr. Maxie Maultsby and other clinical cognitive therapists, we know that there are a number of ways we use language—with ourselves and with others—that are irrational and inaccurate (that is, not based on objective reality and not in our best interests).

Catastrophizing

One of the most common irrational uses of language concerns catastrophizing—the experience that Dan Dean described in Chapter 11.

Here is how it typically happens: You're a salesperson, on your way to have a client sign the biggest contract in your company's history. You're on the freeway, and for whatever reason, you have no cell phone. You're daydreaming about how this deal is going to make your career when you begin to notice that traffic is backing up. Then it stops. Your meeting is in fifteen minutes, you realize that you're going to be late, and now you're beginning to have what we call an "adult tantrum."

Imagine that we can listen in on what you're telling yourself, what you're making up: "I'm going to be late. If I'm late my client will be mad! He won't sign the contract! My boss will go crazy and I could lose my job! The company will go under, but I won't care because I'll be dead already! My family will leave me, my friends will mock me, and I might never work again! *It's a catastrophe!*"

In this state, we tend to blast right past objective reality. The word *catastrophe*—the worst, most awful possible scenario—starts bouncing around in our mind. We quickly escalate a mildly negative experience into disproportionately awful consequences . . . and they are often all made up.

> **W**hen something bad happens, at work or at home, I still worry and catastrophize. What I find really helpful is just talking to my wife, getting a less-emotional perspective on the problem, and discovering what I made up that is not accurate. And that helps tremendously.
>
> —Edwin Peterson, Martin Engineering

How do you challenge "catastrophe maps"? Put yourself back in the same situation. Traffic has ground to a halt. You feel that tantrum building. Instead of giving in to catastrophic thinking, try a variation of Stop, Challenge, and Choose.

THE MINI-MAX TECHNIQUE

▼ **Stop:**

Breathe, calm down, and try to relax. Observe. What is the big picture?
You're fine, you are not going to die, they are not going to take your children
hostage—you're simply stuck in traffic.

▼ **Challenge:**

What is the objective reality? I'm going to be late for my appointment.

What is the worst thing that could happen? Realistically, my client might be
upset that I'm late, but he probably will still sign the contract.

What is the best thing that could happen? My client might also be late for the
meeting and not even notice that I'm late.

What is the most probable thing that could happen? My client will be a little
inconvenienced because I was late, but he's been caught in traffic before, so
he'll understand.

▼ **Choose:**

*Choose an interpretation based on objective and factual data and in your
long-term best interests.* I am not going to get upset over something I can't
control. I'm going to choose to not worry about being late—it is out of my
control—and I'm going to focus on preparing for the meeting.

We call this technique "Mini-Max," putting the minimum and
maximum boundaries around the situation.

Tim Flanagan, a general agent with Mass Mutual in the
Philadelphia area, gives this example of using Mini-Max to challenge his irrational thinking:

*In 1996 I went through the merger of two large organizations.
By most standards, I had a very successful agency, but I also knew*

that they wanted to go from 140 to about 95 agencies. There were 3 agencies in Philadelphia including mine, and we all knew that 1 or 2 of them would have to go. Was I going to be a survivor or not? All sorts of reasons why I might not make the cut—including that I was the oldest general agent—ran through my mind. As the rumors circulated, I became increasingly afraid.

But then I thought, What is the worst thing that could happen to me? Well, I'd be out of a job. That's not good, but it is not as if I was going to die. If I was out of a job, would I be penniless, out on the street? No, we had some assets, we had some income. So I finally got to this: The worst thing that could happen to me in this situation—losing my job—was not all that bad. Fortunately, it didn't happen. But I had a response, I had a plan: I knew I wasn't going to die and life would go on.

"Always," "never," and "the truth"

"All managers are like this." "This always happens." "I never get a break." "This is the truth." "I'm always right and you're always wrong." Statements with absolutes in them are usually inaccurate. They lead to generalized and lazy thinking and tend to calcify our thought processes and stop us from seeing—guess what?—objective reality.

**INSTEAD OF ABSOLUTES,
USE MORE ACCURATE LANGUAGE:**

Be specific! Avoid generalizing. Avoid using the words *always* and *never*. Try using (and thinking with) expressions like "These three salespeople share this 'characteristic.'" "This has happened to me on two occasions." "This is what I made up about this situation." "Under these conditions, this tends to happen."

"I can't"

The literal implication of "I can't" is that something is impossible for me to do. If we think something is impossible, then it is logical to not even try or to try only halfheartedly (because what's the point?). And related to "I can't" is thinking (after trying something once and failing) "I will never understand or master this."

**INSTEAD OF "I CAN'T,"
TRY USING MORE ACCURATE LANGUAGE:**

"This is difficult, possibly very difficult, but not impossible."
"Because I failed the first time, now I am one step closer to understanding and solving the problem."

"I need"

If I don't get what I "need" bad things will happen to me. This implies that I will be in trouble if I don't get what I need. Thinking that I need an "A" on this test (the unexpressed thought being that, if I don't get an "A," something bad will happen) can be a motivator to do whatever it takes to get an "A"—even if it means cheating.

**INSTEAD OF "I NEED,"
USE MORE ACCURATE LANGUAGE:**

"I want" or "I prefer." Most of the time those phrases describe objective reality much more accurately. It usually isn't the end of the world if we don't get what we want.

"It will be awful if . . ."

To the brain, the word *awful* describes a terrible and dreadful consequence, one that "should" be avoided at all costs! Such language conjures up the worst possible scenarios. It creates unnecessary worry, angst, stress, and misery, and it hardly ever meets the test of objective reality: What would a camera see and what are other interpretations?

**INSTEAD OF "IT WILL BE AWFUL,"
USE MORE ACCURATE LANGUAGE:**

The Pecos River secret mantra: "It will be inconvenient if . . ."
The word *inconvenient* can be applied to most difficult situations. It truly helps keep events in perspective and can help stop catastrophizing before it starts:

> It will be inconvenient if I'm late (not a tragedy or the end of the world).
> It will be inconvenient if I miss my flight (ditto).
> It will be inconvenient if I lose my job (ditto).

"That guy is an #@@&(&!!!"

Calling someone a name might be cathartic when we are angry, but it can cause all sorts of escalating problems. Labeling someone is often inflammatory, guaranteed to make the situation worse. Second, by calling someone a #@&*! you've pretty much invalidated his existence—you've demonized him. Your next step is often to dismiss him and his opinions.

> **INSTEAD OF "#@@&(&!!!,"
> USE MORE ACCURATE LANGUAGE:**
>
> If you need to think something "loud" in your brain, think, "That
> guy is an FHB!"—Fallible Human Being—which is an accurate
> and complete definition of most of us. This language will also
> facilitate understanding, acceptance, and forgiveness.

LISTEN AND BE AMAZED

Try this experiment for a day. Listen to how people use inaccurate
language. Observe how some of the worst inaccuracies make you
and others feel: "All XXXs are like that." "It will be *awful* if we
don't get this deal!" "That guy is a $#$I&!!!" "I *need* a drink!"

After just a day of listening to how language is used, you'll soon
pick up that we swim in a sea of irrational thoughts and words, and
they cause all sorts of misunderstandings and unnecessary anxiety,
even fear.

An important ability—one that requires lots of learning and
practice before it becomes automatic—is to use rational, accurate
language. Does our language help us find objective reality? Is our
language helping us think in ways that reflect our best interests?
How we use language—even when we are talking only to
ourselves—is a crucial part of thinking and living rationally.

▼   ▼   ▼

Finding objective reality, using maps in our best interests, using
rational language—these all come down to choosing. Anthro-
pologist Carlos Castañeda, speaking through a fictional character,
Don Juan, wrote, "The trick is what one emphasizes, we either

make ourselves miserable, or we make ourselves strong, the amount of work is the same."

To play to win, or to play not to lose, we begin with a choice. The most powerful choice we can make is to choose our thinking, to choose what we believe based on objective reality and on what is in our best interests. From that choice comes a cascade of other decisions and choices that will help us think and live more rationally and, as we will see in the next part, help us play to win.

PART V

▼▼▼

It takes so much to be a full human being that there are very few who have the enlightenment or the courage to pay the price. One has to abandon altogether the search for security and reach out to the risk of living with both arms. One has to embrace the world like a lover. One has to accept pain as a condition of existence. One has to court doubt and darkness as the cost of knowing. One needs a will stubborn in conflict, but always total acceptance of every consequence of living and dying.

—Morris L. West

Work and Life Strategies

How can we use the tools

of the Results Model and Stop, Challenge, and Choose to help us not only respond more rationally but also thrive in the adventure that is our life?

To help, let's go back to Abraham Maslow. Back in the fifties, Maslow asked a very similar set of questions. He wanted to better understand what made a person "well"—or "thriving," to use our term. The problem was that at the time most of psychology was caught up in dealing

with people who were sick. There was no accepted definition of "well." This sent Maslow on a mission to find and describe what "well" meant.

He began by asking people, "Whom do you know who seems really psychologically healthy?" At first, he got a lot of puzzled looks. So he better defined what he meant: "Whom do you know who fits the following characteristics: the same kinds of things happen to them as to everyone else—good things, bad things, awful things—but they tend to bounce back faster, grow from the experience, and come out of them stronger?"

He got a name here and a name there until he ended up with the famous thirty people— from all walks of life—who became the basis of his most famous work, the Hierarchy of Relative Prepotency (commonly known as the hierarchy of human needs or Maslow's pyramid). He labeled his "well" people "self-actualized." They were motivated out of a desire to actualize— to bring into being and action— their deepest selves. They were also, as Maslow wrote, "involved in a cause outside of their own skin, in something outside of themselves." In Pecos River parlance, we would call them emotionally and spiritually mature— seeking growth, serving a higher cause, and having the emotional ability to bounce back from defeats and actually grow from them (I cannot fail, I can only learn and grow).

> *My investigations on self-actualization . . . did not start out to be research. They started out as the effort of a young intellectual to try to understand two of his teachers whom he loved, adored and admired and who were very, very wonderful people. It was as if they were not quite people, but something more than people. . . . I realized that their patterns could be generalized, I was talking about a kind of person, not about two non-comparable individuals. There was a wonderful excitement to that.*
>
> —Abraham Maslow,
> *The Farther Reaches of Human Nature*

In the second half of *Play to Win!* we are going to propel ourselves toward becoming full human beings and experiencing what Maslow was talking about—being "not quite people, but something more than people." The word, of course, that has been passed down through the millennia to describe the kinds of men and woman who are "something more than people" is *hero*.

THE HERO'S JOURNEY

The stories of those who walk the path of the hero are remarkably the same. Through countless generations and cultures, stories of heroes have been passed down to us to explain

> **A**sk yourself for one moment what your feelings have been on the eve of some act involving courage. . . . Has it not felt something like this? I cannot do this. This is too much for me. I shall ruin myself if I take this risk. I cannot take the leap, it's impossible. All of me will be gone if I do this, and I cling to myself.
>
> —J. N. Figgis

what life is about and what is expected of us. Joseph Campbell, our generation's foremost interpreter of myths and legends, tracked numerous versions of the hero's journey over cultures and back through the ages. The theme he found running through the many legends of the hero goes something like this:

There was this village. In this village people were content and at peace. Life was generally good and had been for many years.

Then one day everything changed. A story spread rapidly through the village that there was a dragon out there! First, it was just a rumor. No one had actually seen a dragon, but everyone knew someone who had. Then their fears were confirmed—it was on CNN—there really was a dragon and it was headed for the village. People panicked! They ran around, children in tow, yelling, "We are all going to die!"

Finally, someone spoke up and said, "What we need is a hero, someone from our village to go out and slay the dragon." So everyone in the village began to look for a hero. After much looking, weighing of options, listening to excuses—lo and behold—they chose Mary.

At first, Mary catastrophized: "Why me? I don't want to go. I'm scared I'll die! I'm comfortable here. I'm no match for a dragon!"

But finally, after stopping and challenging her fears, after some reflection, Mary reluctantly acquiesced, got out of her chair, walked out of the gate of the village, and headed down the path into the forest.

So Mary began her adventure—the endeavor for which the outcome was uncertain. Of course, her journey didn't take her directly to the dragon. There were many challenges she had to face first (eighty-three, in fact). Each challenge was a little bit more than she thought she could handle.

Mary met and overcame the Three Billy Goats Gruff, she outsmarted the Sicilian who told her never to play against a Sicilian

---

THREE TRUTHS

Three things are true about the quest for becoming a full human being. First, we are almost always initially reluctant—we don't want to go. Why change? Life is good and we are comfortable. It's like getting out of a warm bed on a cold morning to go climb a mountain. Comfort and warmth pull at us. Not to mention, it's scary out there—we might fail or be devoured (we're not sure which is worse). But the second truth is this: The way we grow as human beings is to be on the path toward the dragon. In myth, growth requires us to reject comfort and embrace and endure risk, danger, and pain. The third truth: Anyone who is not on the journey is deemed to be asleep—intoxicated by comfort and convenience. When you are asleep, no growth is possible.

when death was on the line. She rescued the handsome prince, lived with him for a few months, and then dumped him because he was so self-involved.

Each challenge was different and it called for different strengths. Each time she was certain that she would fail, but for each challenge she managed to reach deep inside herself to find what was needed to overcome it. She was defeated occasionally, but she persisted (and, obviously, didn't die). As she overcame a challenge, her reward was another challenge, another of her eighty-three problems. But these, too, she overcame. Her confidence grew, her courage grew, her faith that she could now handle anything grew.

Mary was now to the point where she believed that when challenge confronted her she would figure out a way—bridges would appear, doors would open. She now had deep faith in her ability to handle the adventure. She was no longer quite the same person that she was when she began. She was stronger, wiser, more creative, persistent, and courageous. She had learned about herself in ways that would have been impossible had she stayed in the village.

And so Mary came upon the dragon.

Of course, in mythology dragons stand for something else. So it is with the

> **A**nd then suppose that the spirit has conquered and you have done this impossible thing, do you not find afterwards that you possess yourself in a sense that you never had before? That there is more of you? . . . So it is throughout life . . . you know "nothing ventured nothing won" is true in every hour, it is the fibre of every experience that signs itself into the memory.
>
> —J. N. Figgis

dragon that Mary—and all of us—must face if she is to be successful in her journey toward becoming that full human being.

To explain, remember the movie *Return of the Jedi*—a heroic tale
spun for a modern audience. Luke Skywalker, the hero, is training
with Yoda to become a Jedi warrior. Now Luke is a headstrong
young man. He's already growing impatient with the Zen-like mut-
terings of Yoda. Yoda gives Luke this test: He must enter a cave and
defeat the warrior (the dragon) deep within. Yoda tells Luke that it
will be a most difficult and challenging task. Luke, of course, blows
off that warning and enters the cave, there to find Darth Vader.
There is a fierce battle. The fight is a close one, but eventually Luke
prevails. With a final slash of his lightsaber, he cuts off the head—
helmet intact—of his archenemy. The shield to Darth Vader's helmet pops open and what does Luke see? Staring back at him is himself—Luke Skywalker. Luke staggers back, overwhelmed by this
revelation and its meaning.

THE EGO-CENTERED DRAGON

One of the most difficult challenges we each face on our journey is
to have our "ego-centeredness" exposed to the light of day. By *ego-
centered* we don't mean
some complex psycho-
logical idea; rather, we
use the word to describe
one of the hallmarks of
immaturity—believing
that the world and life
revolve around us. It's
just like the old joke:
"Enough about me. What do think about me?"

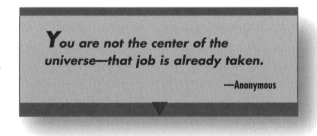

You are not the center of the
universe—that job is already taken.

—Anonymous

Being ego-centered is a part of human development. We go
from being dependent on others for life to eventually being inde-

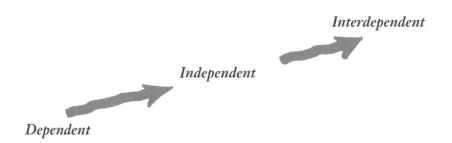

Interdependent

Independent

Dependent

The Growth Model

pendent, able to take care of ourselves. Both of those phases of growth are essentially ego-centered, revolving around "me." When I am dependent, others take care of "me." When I'm independent, I take care of "me." I "look out for #1."

The problem is that it is easy to get stuck in the independence phase. We get stuck in the belief—surrounded often by others and a culture that are also stuck in the belief—that life revolves around "me" and being independent.

In order for Luke to access the full powers of the Jedi, he needed to let go of his ego and trust "the force." In our more prosaic language, as individuals we need to let go of "me" and move on to the most mature level of human develoment—interdependence. Life is about "we."

> **T**he first part of life in Africa with the Maasai is about being a warrior. And nothing would get done if we didn't have warriors and we didn't have people having children, if we didn't have people who were inde-pendent. But as we individuate, we then realize the game is really about fulfillment, which comes from intima-cy and from creative expression.
>
> —Dick Leider, *The Power of Purpose*

Most of us will face our "developmental crossroads" sooner or later. The majority of us will have a crisis that will shake us out of our "life is about me" mental model—the birth of our children, the deaths of our parents, friends, or spouse. All these give us an insight into a deeper and richer vein of what life is about, and these events can push us toward further development.

THE DRAGON'S TREASURE

But the dragon that is our ego-centeredness will battle us all the way. Facing the dragon and taming it is often the most difficult part of the hero's journey. The ego-centered dragon fights—as all dragons do—because it is guarding a secret treasure with its life. It is guarding the answers to the two most important questions being asked of us: Who am I? Why am I here?

The dragon fiercely guards its treasure because, if we see through to who we are and why we are here, it is likely that we will pursue the answers (read *treasure*) with all our hearts. If that happens, all that our ego-centered self craves—to be comfortable, to be #1—will fall away. We will no longer care about simply making "me" comfortable, because we will be in the pursuit of higher meaning.

*I*gnore that man behind the curtain!

—*The Wizard of Oz*

So as our hero Mary faces off to do battle with the egocentric dragon, the dragon is in a battle for its life. But Mary has grown through the adventure. She is not the Mary who began the journey. As a result of her growth—despite all of the dragon's threats and bullying—she sees the dragon for what it truly is, a small and relatively insignificant "tiny terrorist." The dragon that has haunted her throughout her journey is really nothing more than her own ego-centeredness, which she had elevated to dragon status.

There is no final, cataclysmic battle between Mary and her dragon. As soon as Mary sees the dragon for what it is—simply her egocentric self using made-up fears (False Events Appearing Real) to control her—the dragon is tamed and Mary goes on to be her true self and live a meaningful and interdependent life.

▼   ▼   ▼

This is the mythological version—sprinkled heavily with our interpretations—of our developmental journey, a representation of what we must do and what is expected of us if we are to grow into the full human beings we are meant to be. We have to be willing to go on our adventure. We have to be willing to face challenges in order to grow. We have to be willing to face and tame that part of ourselves that believes it is the center of the universe. Finally, we have to pursue the answers to the questions Who am I? Why am I here?

It doesn't matter if you have three kids and a good job. It doesn't matter if you are looking forward to taking it easy now. It doesn't matter if you are in midlife and asking, Is this all there is? The hero's story is about your own path and your own journey. Only you can slay your dragon, and it must be slain if you are to grow. You are either on the journey or you're asleep.

I've Got
Your Name
in My Pocket

Just like Mary, the protagonist in our hero's journey in the last chapter, we make choices, respond to events in our journeys every day—as events occur, as problems need to be solved—

based on wanting to grow or wanting to avoid potential fear or pain. A game we play in our classes illustrates this point.

The objective of "Name in the Pocket" is to pick a partner, go to that person, and do whatever is necessary (within the limits of the game) to make that person your partner. You need to know what you want and go after it.

The game goes like this:

Imagine yourself in a room of thirty people. The trainer gives these instructions: On a note card write down the name of one person in the room whom you would like to get to know better. You can write only one name. Put the card in your pocket.

> **T**hink of life as a process of choices, one after another. At each point there is a progression choice and regression choice. There may be movement towards defense, towards safety, towards being afraid; but over on the other side, there is the growth choice. To make the growth choice instead of the fear choice a dozen times a day is to move a dozen times a day towards self-actualization.
>
> —Abraham Maslow, *The Farther Reaches of Human Nature*

The game begins. You start out toward your Name in the Pocket partner. Immediately, you're hit with the thought—what if she doesn't want to be with me? That slows you down for a second. Then someone else goes up to your potential partner and begins talking. Without missing a beat you make a U-turn and retreat (you don't want everyone to know that you "failed and were rejected"). About that time, someone grabs your arm and tells you that you're the name in his pocket. Feeling a little let down—but relieved that at least you were picked!—you choose to stay with this person. This all happens in a matter of minutes.

Concluding instruction: Take the card out of your pocket. Are you with the person whose name you wrote down? The answer—90 percent of the time—is no.

End of exercise.

As soon as the game starts, we are besieged with ego-centered distractions. "I might be rejected, I might be embarrassed!" More often, we simply automatically react to that early warning radar that says, "Potentially embarrassing situation—avoid!" In the game, most people give up their pursuit too soon and too easily. They play it safe, they play not to lose.

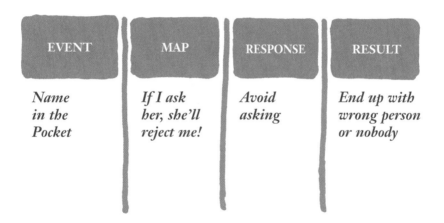

EVENT	MAP	RESPONSE	RESULT
Name in the Pocket	*If I ask her, she'll reject me!*	*Avoid asking*	*End up with wrong person or nobody*

Name in the Pocket can be uncomfortable. It graphically and often painfully demonstrates to participants how we respond to events from the "safety, defense, and avoidance standpoint"—in a phrase, how we play not to lose.

Why? Is it because we don't want to risk embarrassment? We don't want to make a scene? Because it's just a silly game? Because we were taught not to be selfish or assertive? Are these the kinds of phrases that could end on up our tombstone? "Here lies David. He didn't get what he wanted because he feared embarrassment."

FAMOUS NAME IN THE POCKET STRATEGIES:

▼ **Analysis paralysis**

This is the strategy of thinking instead of doing: "Hey, this won't work. Obviously, everyone can't get the partner they want." You never leave your chair and the game passes you by.

▼ **The eighth-grade dance**

"Somebody please pick me!"—and you wait for someone to come and get you.

▼ **U-turn**

You are walking toward Mary. As you approach her, Susan comes up to her and she turns to talk with Susan. Without even breaking stride, you do a U-turn and turn to Frank: "Frank, will you be my partner?" And you think, "Yeah, Frank, will be a great partner. I can learn from him," and "Mary— I didn't need her anyway." (Right!)

▼ **"Thank God" strategy**

You think, "This is going to be a tough exercise and I want her as my partner. I hope she says yes. What if she doesn't want me, what will I do . . . ?" Then another person grabs you, and you hug her and say, "Thank God!"

▼ **"I don't want to hurt you" strategy**

You're going toward Mary, then someone else picks you! "Oh, shucks!"—you really wanted to be with Mary, but if you say no, this other person's feelings will be hurt. He won't like you, may reject you, and you have to work with him (all made-up stuff)—"Okay," you say, "I'll be your partner."

▼ **"Awful-worst fear" strategy**

You make it all the way to Mary and in your most open, vulnerable way you tell her "Your name is on my card." Mary says, "Gee, that is sooo nice . . . but I really wanted to be with Ellen. I need at least to check with Ellen—if she doesn't want to be with me, I'd be delighted to be your partner. You can be my second choice." You walk away saying, "I'm embarrassed to death."

"I MADE A BEELINE FOR BOB"

But what does it look like when someone—which is rare—goes for it and gets what he or she wants? As Wendy Steele, who was then with Coca-Cola, describes her Name in the Pocket experience, it looks like this:

> *I had written down Bob's name immediately and put it in my pocket. When the facilitator said go, I jumped out of my chair. I had already located where Bob was sitting—there were sixty people in a big circle—I made a beeline for him. Bob was at the point where he was rising up out of his chair, but still in the crouched-over, kind of bent-knee position. I made eye contact with him and said, "Bob, I need for you to come with me, we're going to sit in the middle of the room on the floor." I said it just like that, boom, I just said it. And his eyes looked in my eyes, and I thought, "Oh my God, he looks like a deer caught in headlights."*
>
> *To my amazement, he followed me and we sat down on the floor. Then within three or four seconds, another woman approached me, tapped me on the shoulder, bent over, and said, "Wendy, I picked you to be my partner." And I very quickly, matter-of-factly, said, "I'm sorry, it's too late, I've already picked Bob to be my partner." I didn't know where these words were coming from; it's not my style! Then another woman approached from the opposite end of the room, leaned over, and said to Bob, "Bob, I've picked you to be my partner." He, of course, didn't get a chance to speak, because I leaned over and said, "I've already chosen him to be my partner."*
>
> *Then the trainer called time. We were amazed to see that we were the only ones out of sixty people in that room who were paired up. The trainer, bless his heart, said, "People, what happened? This is an exercise in commitment!" And somebody said, "We only had two minutes, and the person I picked picked somebody else, and*

that's really not fair." The trainer said, "What do you mean it's not fair? Is life fair? Are you going to wait for somebody to make something happen for you? What happened?"

Then he asked, "Is there anybody here who agreed to be partners?" And Bob raised his hand. I looked at him, and I didn't believe it! He reached into his pocket and he pulled out his piece of paper, and it had my name on it. There were no words to describe it. Someone asked the trainer if this had ever happened before. He said, "You know, I don't think it ever has."

The punch line, of course, is that within the year Bob and Wendy were married.

▼   ▼   ▼

What Name in the Pocket wonderfully illustrates is what happens at those choice-points described by Maslow. It is a powerful way to catch ourselves being ourselves. We may choose safety—don't go to her because she might reject you—or we may choose growth, as Wendy did. The growth choice *requires* us to risk being rejected, even being embarrassed—emotionally uncomfortable. The price of growth—of getting what we want—is often taking those kinds of risks.

The issue is this: A dozen times a day on our journeys we come to choice-points just like those in Name in the Pocket. We run into obstacles on the path to getting what we want. The obstacles are sometimes real, sometimes largely imagined. But in the face of those obstacles we often give up too easily and too soon. Why? Because what drives the Name in the Pocket game (whether we are playing in the classroom or in life) is the way we decide to handle fear—especially the "False Events Appearing Real" kind of fears guarded by the ego-centered dragon. We call them the Four Fatal Fears.

THE FOUR
FATAL FEARS

The late Dr. W. Edwards Deming, the quality guru and namesake of Japan's prestigious Deming award, was really outspoken on the effect of fear. Deming had fourteen points on how to manage a high-quality organization. Point number eight was that it was the *obligation of management* to drive fear out of the company. He went as far as to say that if management didn't drive fear out of the company, none of his other thirteen points would work.

Deming was talking principally about control management: organizations and managers who use fear—of being fired, of reprisals, of losing status—as their means for managing a company. Deming's belief was that quality, innovation, and creativity all required risk taking and the willingness to speak up. These characteristics are understandably rare in a fear-based organization—where much energy is spent playing politics and covering up mistakes.

Fear works in almost exactly the same way for us as individuals. We cannot be our creative and innovative best—in Maslow's words, "something more than people"—when we operate out of fear.

WHO ARE YOU CALLING AFRAID?

Now, before you think "I'm not afraid," the fears we're talking about are not the kind we experience walking down a dark alley at night or sliding on a slippery road in our car. That kind of fear is a crucial human emotion that evolved to save our skins. Fear is so important to our survival that the perception of potentially fearful events often bypasses the normal perception channels and goes right to that part of the brain that kicks us into action—flee, freeze, or fight.

Without fear and the immediate response it provokes, our species would not have survived. The environment had a way of dealing with the "fearless" biped primate who stood up and asked, "So, what are we making up about leopards?" When everyone else in the tribe was already sprinting for the hills, that thoughtful biped became leopard "lunch meat."

The fears that drive Name in the Pocket and, to a great extent, operate unchecked in many people's lives are more subtle, but they are still powerful. We call them the Four Fatal Fears. They are fatal because—in the face of them—most of us seem to think and respond as if we will die, at least emotionally.

I NEED!

As we wrote in Chapter 12, one of the inaccurate ways we use language in our minds is to believe that we "need" things. The literal definition of "need" is something that is necessary for life. Teenagers, of course, have refined this to a fine art: "Daddy, I need a car. If I don't get one, I'll just die."

Objective reality suggests differently: We *need* very few things to survive as relatively intact, healthy human beings. For example, we need baseline things like air, food, water, shelter, and some human contact. When we say we need anything else or we will die, we are being inaccurate—we are making it up.

Four "I needs" generally run rampant in our minds to create the Four Fatal Fears: to succeed, to be right, to be accepted, and to be comfortable.

THE FOUR FATAL FEARS:

I fear failure: I need to succeed.

I fear being wrong: I need to be right.

I fear rejection: I need to be accepted.

I fear being emotionally uncomfortable: I need to be comfortable.

Evolutionary psychologists study how human psychology has evolved. They would tell us that the Four Fatal Fears were just as crucial to our survival two million years ago as was that "Here comes the leopard! Run!" kind of fear. A lone human had a very small chance of surviving in the hostile "ancestral" environments; however, in groups and tribes we thrived. As a result, over millions of years, our psychology adapted to keep us together in hierarchically structured hunter-gatherer tribes—which was the organizing unit for almost all of the 100,000 generations or so of our existence as a species. The Four Fatal Fears were the kind of anxieties that helped glue the tribe together. They might not have made us happy, but they helped keep us together, alive, and passing on our genes.

But there was a glitch.

> **W**hatever the ancestral environment was like, it wasn't much like the environment we're in now. We aren't designed to stand on crowded subway platforms, or to live in suburbs next door to people we never talk to, or to get hired or fired, or to watch the evening news. This disjunction between the contexts of our design and of our lives is probably responsible for much psychopathology, as well as much suffering of a less dramatic sort.
>
> —Robert Wright, *The Moral Animal*

Even though it is a very recent change in evolutionary terms, we no longer live in hunter-gatherer tribes, and we no longer need to spend most of our waking moments worrying about being accepted and having high status. We are no longer in jeopardy of dying if we are rejected. (But try telling that to your teenager!) In an evolutionary sense, the Four Fatal Fears are maladaptive. That is to say, they are inaccurate and incomplete—albeit deeply held—interpretations. They don't help us thrive in today's world.

FATAL FEAR #1: FEAR OF FAILURE

A friend sat his two kids—ten and thirteen—down and asked them what they thought winning meant. They both piped up with answers right in line with our cultural "We have to *win!*" norm: Winning means beating other people, being the best, being perfect, getting straight "A's," always being first—in short, everything. A moment passed. His ten-year-old daughter then started to cry. She said, "Daddy, I've never been a winner at anything. I've never been the best at anything." Her dad was shocked. His response was to declare that winning in their home—from that point forward— would always be defined as doing your best, not being the best.

This is not an attack on competition! Being competitive is a good thing. For example, competitive sports for kids are a wonderful teaching ground for important values and wisdom. Kids can learn that working hard pays off, that we gain strength through training and work, that competition can bring out our best, not our worst. They can learn persistence when they are losing, to follow the rules (that is, to stick to values and ethics) under pressure, to stay calm when everyone is upset.

THE PLAYING NOT TO LOSE STRATEGY:

To see how, in our "Must be a winner!" culture, we play not to lose, think about our friend's ten-year-old daughter. If she internalizes the message that winning is everything and losing is to be avoided, the strategy becomes clear. It no longer is about "doing your best," it is about selecting "safe" situations where winning or losing is not on the line: Pick your occupation and your relationships based on the assurance that you will win or look like a winner. Don't take real risks where winning or losing is involved. Play it safe.

Thinking "I need to win or be seen as a winner above all else" can, however, create all sorts of dysfunctional behavior. Our culture is full of examples of people having adult tantrums because they lose—if I lose it will be a catastrophe!

FATAL FEAR #2: FEAR OF BEING WRONG

In the middle of an argument with our spouse or loved one, when we belatedly discover that we are in the wrong, do we admit it? OF COURSE NOT! In the heat of an argument our ego craves being right. We are often more willing to do damage to a relationship by arguing than to admit that we were wrong.

THE PLAYING NOT TO LOSE STRATEGY:

Avoid situations where your intelligence might truly be tested, where you might not know the answers. Stay within the bounds of what you know. Don't take the risk of being wrong. Never admit that you made a mistake or that you are wrong.

FATAL FEAR #3: FEAR OF REJECTION

Being rejected—thrown out of the tribe—was probably a death sentence for our ancient ancestors, and the fear of rejection still infects our thinking. The classic example happens in high school. Think of it from the perspective of a teenage boy: You want to ask this girl out. It's early evening, the time has come, you go to the phone, stare at it, and then decide to make a sandwich. Sandwich eaten, you go back to the phone, dial the number. She answers and you hang up. Why? Because you're making stuff up: When you ask her out, she'll

THE PLAYING NOT TO LOSE STRATEGY:

Avoid situations where you risk not being accepted! It's always better (the ego-centered self tells you) to settle for less than to be rejected. Being rejected will feel worse than awful! At work, it is better to not speak up, to not go against the group, rather than risk being rejected and ostracized. ("You geek," they might think.)

laugh and tell you, "What were you thinking? You're a geek!" Then she'll hang up on you and call all her friends, and they'll all laugh. Then they'll call all *their* friends, share the cosmic joke, and eventually it will end up on the Internet and you'll have to leave the country, broken and humiliated. So you decide not to call (and pray that she calls you).

FATAL FEAR #4: FEAR OF EMOTIONAL DISCOMFORT

This one is really a grab bag of anxieties: Never allow yourself into situations where you might be embarrassed; never show vulnerability; never look foolish; never ask for help, because asking for help is a sign of weakness.

In a seminar a manager recalled that when he was eleven years old he knew that he must have done something terribly wrong because his father had stopped hugging and kissing him. It wasn't until later that he realized that the cause was his father's "map": His father believed that showing emotion and displays of affection toward anyone over the age of eleven was a sign of a weak charac-

THE PLAYING NOT TO LOSE STRATEGY:

Avoid all potentially embarrassing situations or situations where
you might lose emotional control. Don't try new things (at least
in public) because you might look foolish and be "embarrassed
to death." Always practice new dances at home, in the closet in
the dark where no one can see you. It is better to be an expert
than a learner—learners are always trying new things and
making mistakes.

ter. For his dad, intimacy with his son was embarrassing. So his dad
made the choice to clamp down on his feelings and avoid intimacy.

▼　▼　▼

The naturalist Robert Ingersoll observed that in nature there
are no rewards or punishments, just consequences. When we
choose to avoid the Four Fatal Fears, we guarantee ourselves that
when we come to those dozen choice-points a day we are going to
choose the path of safety and not growth. When we consistently
choose—day in and day out—the path of safety and defense, it
becomes more than a series of choices. The *consequence* is that playing not to lose becomes a life strategy—a complete plan for how we
want to run our life and how we want it all to turn out.

PLAYING NOT TO LOSE

The Playing Not to Lose epitaph: I survived. I didn't get hurt. I was comfortable. I was never lost. I was always right. I never really knew who I was (or who I could have become).

> *The most fundamental assumption of the underground managerial world is that the truth is a good idea when it is not embarrassing or threatening—the very conditions under which it is especially needed.*
>
> —Chris Argyris, Overcoming Organizational Defenses

When we are deeply invested in playing not to lose, we often catch ourselves thinking—and it seems almost rational—"If I can just get to my death unscathed, I'll have made it!" When we are deeply invested in safety and comfort, playing not to lose becomes our life strategy. As the game we are playing, playing not to lose is composed of four elements that run our thinking and show up in the way we make choices and respond to the events in our lives: philosophy, core maps, an interpretation template, and responses.

MANUFACTURER'S WARNING!

In the following, we are going to take playing not to lose to the extreme for illustration purposes only. In reality, most of us call upon different maps and responses, depending on the situation. For example, at home, we might see our family as loving, trustworthy, and caring, and we might see work as a winner-take-all, take-no-prisoners battleground for scarce resources. Or vice versa.

PHILOSOPHY: LIFE IS ABOUT SURVIVAL

When we are deeply involved in playing not to lose, we are motivated to survive emotionally, to not get hurt. An event happens and our early warning system immediately begins to ask questions:

How can I best protect myself from harm? What is the best way to avoid experiencing any of the Four Fatal Fears?

The flip side of trying to avoid pain is that we are seeking—as a priority—comfort and convenience. For example, we are more likely to avoid telling the truth if it involves short-term pain, because it is much more convenient and "short-term comfortable" to not tell the truth.

CORE MAPS: SCARCITY AND "NO TRUST"

I want to emotionally survive, and that's tough to do because resources are scarce and I can't trust anyone. Scarcity and no trust. These represent the core maps of playing not to lose.

Scarcity is a map that says there are not enough resources—money, jobs, or love and the like—to go around. Therefore, life is inherently competitive. From this perspective, we see people as greedy (wanting what is ours). We see life as a battle with others to get what we believe we deserve. Because we are in a competitive battle for resources, we are suspicious of people. People can't be trusted until they prove they can be trusted ... over and over again.

INTERPRETATION TEMPLATE: THE FOUR FATAL FEARS

The Four Fatal Fears form the template for interpreting events when we adopt the play not to lose strategy. As a result,

> **A** common core map of abused kids (and the occasional senior executive) is "Everybody is out to get you, you've got to be tough, I'm going to screw you over before you screw me over."
>
> —Tracy Burke, M.S.W.

we respond in a way that helps us avoid failing, being wrong, being rejected, or being emotionally uncomfortable.

PLAYING NOT TO LOSE RESPONSES

How we respond to events is where the rubber meets the road, how we influence the results we get in our lives. When we are playing not to lose, we tend to respond to events in five ways.

1. Self-protection and self-promotion

How can I best protect myself and promote my agendas and what I "need" above all else? This is the expression of that ego-centered self taking care of #1.

Self-promotion and self-protection are like the pufferfish, which blows itself up like a balloon in order to look larger and more menacing. When we self-protect and self-promote, we do essentially the same thing. Our ideas are the important ones, and our needs and our crises are the most serious ones. We are the center of attention.

> *It's amazing—a lot of times I'll go into a meeting and there'll be four or five people on the same level and there'll be a boss. If you can step back, you'll see a tremendous amount of competition among players for share of voice during a meeting. There is one-upmanship, what I'm doing versus the other one. How can I look better than everyone else? It is all about making stuff up about what the leader wants and about your behavior in that meeting. Everyone is coming in with their own political agenda.*
>
> —Paul Ruane, Schering-Plough HealthCare

2. Stay in your comfort zone

We each have a comfort zone, a set of behaviors and ways

of thinking that are habitual. We drive to work the same way every day, we associate with the same people, we do the same work, we have our normal work and meeting behaviors—they are comfortable and safe. When we are invested in playing not to lose, we make up that if we take a risk we might get hurt. Therefore, we stay inside our comfort zone, with what we know, with whom we know, and with our habits.

Think about it. How many of us routinely dive into new experiences, or relish being the learner, the mistake maker, the joyous tourist (Wow, look at that!)? How many of us are comfortable with passionately voicing an idea one minute and the next readily admitting that we were wrong? How many of us, in search of the truth, happily give up long-held assumptions when faced with new and different information? How many of us actively seek information that challenges our long-held assumptions? Not many of us. More commonly—when we are playing not to lose—we avoid anything that pushes us out of our comfort zone.

3. Irrational thinking

The futurist Marshall McLuhan wrote that we drive into the future looking in the rearview mirror. When we play not to lose, we tend to make choices and decisions based on what has happened to us in the past, without stopping and challenging whether our choice is rational or relevant. We tend to react emotionally without checking out our thinking or challenging our maps.

4. A closed mind

A closed mind believes that admitting that we can learn something new, or that we don't understand, is a sign of weakness. We would rather be right; we need to be seen as the expert in order to protect our sense of infallibility. We would much prefer to be the expert than the learner.

When we play not to lose, we have closed our minds to anything new, to anything innovative, and especially to anything different.

> **B**ecause many professionals are always successful at what they do, they rarely experience failure. And because they have rarely failed, they have never learned how to learn from failure. So whenever their . . . strategies go wrong, they become defensive, screen out criticism, and put the "blame" on anyone and everyone but themselves. In short, their ability to learn shuts down precisely at the moment they need it most.
>
> —Chris Argyris, "Teaching Smart People How to Learn"

5. Blame others

When we are invested in self-promotion and self-protection, appearing fallible is very painful. We tend to blame others, deny responsibility, or play victim (he did it, she did it, it did it, they did it to me.) We will go to great lengths to shift blame or rationalize it away: it could have happened to anyone, it's not really my fault. In a recent drunk-driving case in New Mexico, the defendant claimed that it wasn't his fault that his blood alcohol level was twice the legal limit; his body metabolized sugar into alcohol. (The donuts made me drunk.) Each of us has a subtle voice that tries to weasel us out of being the cause of mistakes and bad things. Our ego-centered selves need to appear infallible.

COMFORT, CONVENIENCE, AND RELIEF

What are the results we tend to get when we play not to lose? We get what we pay attention to. When our life is about seeking comfort, convenience, and relief, those are the results we have a high probability of producing. We have a good shot at looking like a winner, being accepted, being right, and staying emotionally comfortable. We can arrive at the end and think, "I made it unscathed,

PHILOSOPHY	CORE MAPS	INTER-PRETATION TEMPLATE	RESPONSES
Playing Not to Lose			
Emotional survival	*Scarcity and no trust*	*Avoid being wrong, being rejected, failing, and being emotionally uncomfortable*	*1. Self-protection and self-promotion* *2. Stay inside your comfort zone* *3. Irrational thinking* *4. A closed mind* *5. Blame others*

unhurt, and I stayed comfortable—I was never embarrassed—I won!"

If you are asking—as we all do occasionally—what is wrong with comfort, relief, and convenience, there are two answers. First, when we choose the path of playing not to lose, behind us lie all those other paths that point toward growth. We eliminate hosts of possibilities. By choosing to belong, to not make waves, we eliminate finding our voice. Our voice atrophies because it is not used. By choosing to never be wrong, we eliminate intellectual growth, because it requires experimenting and risking being wrong. If we choose to be comfortable above all else, we eliminate those choices that require us to endure discomfort for higher causes, values, and meaning—and of course our courage and creativity atrophy. When we play not to lose, we choose a narrow and confining path—but it is safe.

▼   ▼   ▼

But part of us will always rebel. That's the other problem with playing not to lose: We understand, at a deep level, that our life is not simply about avoiding pain, difficulty, and seeking comfort. We know there is more.

We find ourselves in midlife bored and asking, "Is this all there is?" We seem lost. "In the middle of my life I found myself in the deep woods, lost," Dante wrote in *The Inferno*. We find ourselves wondering about the point of working another day only to go home, sleep, get up, and do it all over again. We're depressed, anxious—we're distracted. We dream—or we interpret our dreams—in a way that seems to point us in new directions. These anxieties often lead to fear or existential depression (besides my existence being meaningless, I'm having no fun and I can *feel* the clock ticking).

You don't have to be lost. Instead, these anxieties can become the opening, the awakening, the call to begin your journey to find your true self. We must use words to describe this path—and words are terribly limiting. They cannot begin to describe the uniqueness and the power of being on your journey.

We describe the journey of growth as playing to win.

CHOOSING GROWTH

T he Playing to Win epitaph: I took the risk. I discovered who I was. I changed. I grew. I learned. I was an adventurer.

At its simplest, playing to win is consciously using Stop, Challenge, and Choose to make growth choices instead of fear or avoidance choices. For example, at work you need to become—finally—computer literate in order to compete with the twenty- and thirty-somethings to whom computers are like telephones. Admitting that you need to learn and then setting out on the path of learning means that you will make a number of mistakes—publicly—before you become competent. You will need to ask for help—"What happens when I send a document to print?" "What's an operating system?"

> *E*very blade of grass has its Angel that bends over and whispers, Grow, grow.
>
> —The Talmud

You come up to the choice-point. Playing not to lose would be avoiding asking for help and learning because you don't want to be wrong, appear fallible, or be embarrassed. (Of course, you can't learn computers and networking by osmosis!) The playing to win response would be to stop and challenge your fear-based thinking: What is more important, learning the skill or avoiding being embarrassed? Playing to win, ultimately, is choosing to try—you choose the growth path.

Playing to win is also a life strategy and Stop, Challenge, and Choose is the tool you can use to implement that strategy. As a life strategy, playing to win also has a philosophy, core maps, a template for interpreting events, and a set of responses, but they are nothing like the elements that defined playing not to lose.

PHILOSOPHY: LIFE IS GROWTH

What is my life about? It is about growing up, about going as far as I can with all that I have. The bedrock belief that underlies playing to win is that life is about emotional, intellectual, and spiritual growth. What can I become? Why am I here and how can I serve? These are the questions that prompt us when we are playing to win, that push us toward becoming who we are meant to be and toward interdependence. Life is seen as a difficult—but not impossible—series of challenges that call us to grow.

I've made some really significant changes in my life in the last few years. I decided to start over, which really required me to get out of my comfort zone—totally. But at some point I decided that I just didn't want to be afraid anymore.

I asked myself what I really wanted in my life. Another part was seeing my grandmother in her nineties. When she was eighty-seven she was going to college at Oxford! I didn't want find myself at her age wondering "What if?" I got that I was in charge of my destiny.

At British Airways in the Bulova Building, which is covered with signs about playing to win, one says, "A journey of a thousand miles begins with a single step." That really summed it up for me and now there is no turning back.

—Sarah DiGiorgio, British Airways

CORE MAPS: ABUNDANCE AND TRUST

Life is difficult, but I have all the resources—including my own courage and creativity—required to grow. Since my life is about me growing up, I am not in competition with anyone else.

There is an abundance of resources. There are more than enough of the resources that matter—relationships, love, opportu-

> **P**eople are intelligent, creative, adaptive, self-organizing and meaning-seeking.
>
> —Margaret Wheatley and Myron Kellner-Rogers, *A Simpler Way*

nities to grow, jobs, money, and so on. From this "map" of the how the world works (based on what we've been told by the people we trust and personal experience) people are seen not as greedy but more often as "needy." They often need support, clarity, help, trust, and confidence, but there are commonly all sorts of communication problems that block us from coming together in meaningful ways. Further, given that people are not out to get what is ours, people can be trusted, until they demonstrate that they can't be.

INTERPRETATION TEMPLATE: AS FAR AS I CAN WITH ALL THAT I HAVE

When we play not to lose, events are filtered through our need to avoid the Four Fatal Fears. When we are playing to win, we interpret events this way: How can I go as far as I can with all that I have—regardless of whether it might put me in jeopardy of experiencing failure, being rejected, and so on?

PLAYING TO WIN RESPONSES

Because I want to go as far as I can with all that I have, I tend to choose to respond to events—especially the challenging and important ones—consciously with the following six responses.

1. I will base my truth on objective reality

This is clearly the baseline commitment of playing to win, and it is a difficult one. A crucial premise of this book is that you must search for objective reality and absorb it, hold on to it as you would a life jacket in a stormy sea. Challenge assumptions, check out what you and others are making up, tell the truth as you see it—at least to yourself. Without the commitment to tell yourself the truth, it is nearly impossible to go as far as you can, because you will never really know where you are. You will have minor setbacks and deceive yourself into thinking it is as far as you can go. You will have bad days that you'll tell yourself are catastrophic. The truth will set you free. It usually makes you miserable first, but committing to telling yourself the truth is the prerequisite for growth.

> *I have to be able to look at myself in the mirror and know that what I am doing is the right thing. Second, I have to be able to look into the eyes of the individuals being impacted by my decision—whether family or the people at work—and know that what I am doing is the right thing. They might not agree with what I am doing. But I am not going to shirk away from being honest with myself and being straight with the people I'm involved with.*
>
> —John Marshall, Dofasco Steel

2. I will make choices rationally

When we are honest with ourselves, we are much more capable of making rational choices. Billy Weisman, president and CEO of Weisman Enterprises, Inc., wrote a set of values for his multi-million-dollar management company by creating the acronym SOAR: Supportive—Objective—Accountable—Responsive.

In many companies, decisions are too often tainted by old maps. Objectivity for us is getting accurate observations and honest feed back, which leads to unbiased decision making. It is a product of listening with an open mind and placing genuine value on all input. Do not prejudge. If we want to make honest decisions, we get there by being objective. It creates much better decisions and it helps eliminate politics.

Thinking rationally is the crux. You come up to one of those choice-points. Are you going to make your decisions based on old maps? Or are you going to challenge your irrational thinking, are you going to have the courage to ask questions: What is objective reality here? How do I want this situation to turn out? Thinking rationally is how we most often stay on track, stay calm, and thus are able to make playing to win choices more often.

> **O**ne of the major differentiations between success and failure—across the board—is the failure to commit to excellence, the acceptance of mediocrity. Our vision is to go where no person has gone before. That sounds very familiar, because it is, but it's fun! We're going to a place that has been uncharted, we have to have the courage to try things, and to leap forward. We're constantly challenging the status quo of how we're doing things.
>
> —Rob Knapp, Merrill Lynch

3. I will give it my personal best

When you play to win, you commit to excellence, personally and professionally. This goes beyond meeting goals or defeating the competition. Goals are made up; they are largely inaccurate and incomplete measures of performance. They can stretch you and inspire you (and competition can make you work harder), but goals are not ends in themselves, they are merely guideposts that point toward "personal best" performance. Being committed to giving your personal best means going beyond your internal or external goals—it means striving to go beyond all previously recognized boundaries.

> **I** do not intend to pause, or rest, or rust.
>
> —Dr. George Sheehan, 60-year-old marathoner

4. I will get out of my comfort zone

How can you tell that you are giving your personal best? A defining ability is the willingness to get outside of your comfort zone—to be comfortable being uncomfortable.

In the Stephen Sondheim musical *Sunday in the Park with George*, a third-generation artist—George—is struggling with his work. He is successful, driven, but not happy. In one scene, George is showing his latest creation, "Chromolume #7," the seventh in a series of towers of lasers and chrome. Up to George comes the critic Blair, who says to him, "George, Chromolume #7? I was hoping for a series of three or four at most . . . but now they simply are becoming more and more about less and less . . . there are new discoveries to be made, George."

George was successful and comfortable. He was secure in what he was doing and producing—he could have continued doing it

> **T**o push oneself to one's limits inevitably involves risk, otherwise they wouldn't be one's limits. This is not to say that you deliberately try something you know you can't do. But you do deliberately try something which you are not sure you can do.
>
> —Woodrow Wilson Sayre

forever. Being liked, being successful, not failing in front of the art world were keeping him inside his comfort zone. The critic Blair represented that deeper voice, the truth that he had been avoiding: Being emotionally comfortable was keeping him from being creative.

Living creatively and courageously requires us to get outside of our comfort zones. We need to be comfortable being uncomfortable, balancing on the very edge of losing control, of failure, of not understanding what we are doing. It is out there that discoveries are made and life is fully lived.

Outside of our comfort zone we feel excited, anxious, passionate, energetic, and alive. We are on the edge of our personal or professional abilities. We don't know how it's going to turn out. It's uncomfortable! But being comfortable being uncomfortable—on that edge—is what is required to truly play to win, to go as far as you can.

We teach our scientists to make a lot of mistakes—we call them experiments—and that those mistakes would turn into positive things. Go off and screw up and you'll learn from it. But we don't teach ourselves that and you don't find that crucial lesson about learning in corporations.

—Bob Root, ORION Learning

5. I cannot fail, I can only learn and grow

When I am focused on learning, I see failure and mistakes in a new light. When we are committed to learning, failures and mistakes have value, because it is through them that learning happens.

And the most important learning we undertake is emotional resilience, the ability to bounce back faster after setbacks, to be able to more effectively push through difficult times. By taking risks, by experiencing pain and fear and getting through it, we grow. Søren Kierkegaard, the Danish Christian philosopher, wrote that there were two kinds of people: those who suffered and those who were professors of the fact that someone had suffered. What he didn't add—but which we all know—is that those who suffer often grow emotionally to a level commensurate with their level of suffering, if they choose to learn. Those who avoid situations where suffering or emotional pain might be an outcome will have a difficult time learning or growing. Evident. Obvious. An athlete who trains only to the point that he or she begins to sense that pain might be on its way will never get stronger or build endurance. To build emotional strength and endurance, we need to go through pain, we need to suffer a little. The more difficult, out-of-comfort-zone experiences we have, the larger, wiser, and more emotionally resilient we become—if we choose to learn.

> **E**ven the wild choices we make are important if we learn from them.
>
> —Helen Mills, Aon Consulting

6. I will take accountability for how I respond

The Results Model rests on the idea that we cannot control the events of our lives. We cannot, then, be accountable for what happens to us, for the events of our lives. Good things happen, bad things happen, tragedies happen. Life is capricious. Oscar Wilde wrote that "life is terribly deficient in form. Its catastrophes happen in the wrong way and to the wrong people." But the power—the freedom and the responsibility—of the Results Model is this: Whether consciously or unconsciously, we make choices about how we respond to those events. Because we have the freedom to make choices, we are by definition accountable for our choices. If we are competent adults, we are accountable for how we choose to respond

> **T**he best way out is through.
>
> —Carl Sandburg

to the events of our lives.

Because we all make bad choices, because we all live with often terrible mistakes and even tragedies caused by how we responded, we don't like this truth. Choice is often difficult, and we are fallible human beings. But simply knowing that at every moment we have a choice in how to respond instead of thinking that we are simply victims—and that we are accountable for that choice—is powerful wisdom that cannot help but grow us.

PHILOSOPHY	CORE MAPS	INTER-PRETATION TEMPLATE	RESPONSES
Playing to Win			
Emotional and spiritual growth	*Abundance and trust*	*Going as far as I can with all that I have and learning from whatever happens*	1. *Base truth on objective reality* 2. *Make decisions rationally* 3. *Give personal best* 4. *Outside comfort zone* 5. *Can't fail, can only learn and grow* 6. *Take accountability*

▼ ▼ ▼

Objective truth, personal best, out of your comfort zone, rational choices, learning, and accountability—this is not easy stuff. So the question is why? Why should you play to win, go as far as you can? Why should you choose this admittedly more difficult path? Why should you not simply surrender to the path of convenience and comfort, the path that most seem to travel? The answer lies in the results you are playing for.

YOU BET
YOUR LIFE!

L ike Stop, Challenge, and Choose,
our choice of life strategy—play to
win or play not to lose—is not compli-
cated stuff. Rather, it is a simple way to
view the decisions and choices we make

every day and the consequences of those choices. The choice depends on what kind of results you want in your life: What do you want your life to be about?

THE GAME IS GAMBLING

Wanting results and getting the results you want, of course, are two different things. Ultimately, life is a gamble: You pick a path and you hope for the best. Choosing a life strategy is gambling, and the stakes are our lives.

So let's imagine for the next few pages that you've walked into a casino where only two games are played—both variations on a

Choose Your Game

Table 1. Playing Not to Lose	Table 2. Playing to Win
PRIZES	PRIZES
Being right	*Truth*
Success	*Growth*
Being in control	*Fun*
Being accepted	*Curiosity*
Comfort	*Healthy relationships*
Convenience	*Joy*
	Understanding
	Better health
	Love
	Fulfillment

larger game called You Bet Your Life. There are two tables with games in progress. At the first table the game is Playing Not to Lose; at the other table it is Playing to Win.

If you've ever gambled, you know that the first rule is that the house always wins because the house isn't gambling; it's taking money off the top. In this game the house is life, and it doesn't give a whit which table you choose, because it's always going to win. Eventually—no matter which game you play—life will win all your time. It will get every minute, every year, until it has taken your whole life. In the end you die—no matter what game you've committed your life to, no matter which core maps you've followed, or whether you got those big deals. Life—the house—gets it all in the end.

The second rule of the game is that you're *gambling*. You can play at one table all your life and all you are assured of is the *possibility* of winning. If you play at the Playing Not to Lose table, you have the *possibility* of winning comfort, relief, or acceptance—but never the guarantee. If you sit at the Playing to Win table, you have the *possibility* of winning growth, health, and joy—but no guarantee. We're talking probabilities, possibilities, and maybes here. In either variation of You Bet Your Life, you place your bets, the house takes its cut, maybe you win what you're playing for and maybe you don't.

ONE GAME AT A TIME

Each of us chooses our game and we invest our time, our days and decades. And we can't play both games at once. If you sit down at the Playing Not to Lose table, you can't win the prizes in the pot at the Playing to Win table. In the same way, if you sit down at the Playing to Win table, if you believe that your life is about growth, balance, health, relationships, and joy, then you probably will sacrifice the prizes of the other table.

THE "GAMES" AT A GLANCE:

	Playing Not to Lose	Playing to Win
Philosophy	Emotional survival	Emotional and spiritual growth
Core maps	Scarcity and no trust	Abundance and trust
Interpretation template	Avoid being wrong, being rejected, failing, and being emotionally uncomfortable	Going as far as I can with all that I have
Responses	1. Self-protection and self-promotion 2. Stay inside your comfort zone 3. Irrational thinking 4. A closed mind 5. Blame others	1. Base truth on objective reality 2. Make decisions rationally 3. Give personal best 4. Outside comfort zone 5. Can't fail, can only learn and grow 6. Take accountability
Results	Being right Being successful Being in control Being accepted Comfort Convenience	Truth Growth Fun Curiosity Relationships Joy Better health Understanding

The price you pay for growth is the risk of failure, not being accepted, being uncomfortable. If you choose spending time with your family, you often need to sacrifice putting in the time to be accepted by the "high-status" work group. You can't work seventy-hour weeks forever, come home tense, tired, and already impatient with your kids, and expect to have healthy family relationships. In the same way, if you are playing for truth, you often have to sacrifice buying into the "consensus hypnosis" of some group—a work team, a corporation, a community. We choose the table that offers the possibility of winning the prizes we most desire.

> *They chose their paths not because they were easy, but because they were difficult.*
>
> —Mary Doria Russell, *The Sparrow*

The choice is rarely an easy one. Most people want to be accepted, to appear successful, to win, *and* to grow, be healthy, and enjoy good relationships. The game becomes interesting in the defining moments of your life when you realize you cannot play both games simultaneously, when you have to choose between them. Then the question becomes what are you going to bet your life on?

EVERY DAY WE MAKE THE CHOICE

We have all been faced with a life-defining choice: Am I choosing this because I need to be accepted, to be successful, to remain comfortable, or to be right? Am I choosing because I want to grow, to maintain relationships, and to seek the truth? The choice of which game you want to play is there every day. Emotional maturity means consciously choosing which game you want to play. Emotional maturity means using Stop, Challenge, and Choose:

What am I making up? What do I really want my life to be about? How will this decision affect my life and the lives of the people I care for? Which game do I want to play?

INTEGRITY OR CONVENIENCE?

Another way to make a conscious choice for growth is to ask, "Am I making a choice for integrity or convenience?" At Pecos River, we define *integrity* as behavior that is in line with our values. Agreeing intellectually with Playing to Win values is easy. Who doesn't believe that giving our personal best is a good thing? This isn't the point, though.

> **E**verything is sweetened by risk.
>
> —Alexander Smith, *Of Death and the Fear of Dying*

Having integrity is putting the truth into practice, having our behavior line up with what we believe. Therein lies the work. Playing to win takes effort, commitment, and risk. Playing not to lose is convenient and avoids pain. Playing to win is hard, tough, frustrating, and painful—instant gratification doesn't exist.

Compounding the difficulty is the dilemma that we live in a culture—as fish swim in the water—that praises and glorifies ease, comfort, and convenience as cultural states of grace. Why struggle to find ourselves, when it is so easy to be merely consumers, whose toughest daily decisions are about where to park, where to go to lunch, what to watch on TV?

▼   ▼   ▼

It is up to you. The game is You Bet *Your* Life. Are you going to play to win or play not to lose? Are you going to choose integrity or convenience? Maslow wrote that our lives are a collection of the dozens of choices we make every day. So today, which game are you going to play? Today, when faced with one of those dozen choice-points, one that will define who you are, how are you going to choose? What is your life really about?

In these plethoric times when there is too much coarse stuff for everybody and the struggle for life takes the form of competitive advertisement and the effort to fill your neighbor's eye, there is no urgent demand for personal courage, sound nerves or stark beauty, we find ourselves by accident. Always before this time the bulk of the people did not overeat themselves because they couldn't, whether they wanted to or not, and all but a very few were kept "fit" by unavoidable exercise and personal danger. Now, if only he pitch his standards low enough, and keep free from pride, almost anyone can achieve a sort of excess. You can go through contemporary life fudging and evading, indulging and slacking, never really hungry nor frightened nor passionately stirred, your highest moment a mere sentimental orgasm and your first real contact with the primary and elemental necessities the sweat of your deathbed.

—H. G. Wells

PART VI

▼▼▼

The Spiritual Adventure

If we choose to play

not to lose as a life strategy, it is the sweat of our deathbed that wakes us up to the fact that we missed our lives. We were so busy "surviving" that we invested too little in growth. That awareness at that moment is pain beyond endurance, because then it is too late. This fact can either frighten you—as death does us all—and you can avoid thinking about it, or you can allow the inevitability of your death to inspire you every day so that you can look back at the end of the adventure and know you pushed your limits, left a legacy, and lived with courage and creativity—you played to win.

If we choose that path, if we absorb the philosophy that life is about growth, we will take playing to win into the deepest realm that we can experience—answering those two critical questions: Who am I? Why am I here?

This journey began for me—professionally and personally—in 1984. I had decided to move from Minneapolis to Santa Fe, New Mexico. I had signed a contract for a book, but I had no idea what to write about. Remedy: vacation and procrastinate. I took three weeks off and went to the Cayman Islands to wait for enlightenment to strike, but there were no ideas, no breakthroughs, nothing, *nada*.

Then in the second week of that trip, with my brain pretty much bleached out from the sun, the first strange twist in this story occurred. I woke up in the middle of the night after a most vivid dream. I got up and wrote down what I had dreamed.

Many years ago, a prince was born in the Land of Abundance. He was a favorite of the gods, so they deemed that he could have anything he wanted by asking for it in the simple and easy way they had provided.

Because the prince was only

a baby, they wanted to be sure that he was protected from danger, so they gave him a servant whose name was Ego. Ego's purpose was to do everything in his power to ensure that the prince wasn't put at risk or harmed in any way.

Ego took his job very seriously. So seriously that he decided that the best way to provide protection was to keep the prince from making any decisions at all. So Ego decided to make all the decisions.

Before long, Ego the servant had become Ego the master.

Soon, the protecting arms of Ego had become a prison for the prince. Yet the prince was so young that he thought this was the way it was supposed to be. Then the gods looked down and they were disappointed. So they granted the prince a single second of insight. And he understood that he had to let go of Ego the master and bring Ego the servant back. He rediscov-

ered the simple and easy way of getting everything he wanted.

He then discovered that what gave him the most pleasure was helping others discover the simple and easy way to get what they wanted, for he had discovered that everyone was born a prince or a princess.

I had no idea what the dream meant, but I was intrigued by the themes of the ego, the prince, and the stroke of insight. Without thinking more about it, I flew to Santa Fe and moved into our new home and office. On the second day, my mail and phone messages caught up with me.

They were all work related except for a message from Bart Regan, one of my closest friends in high school. I got Bart on the phone and the first thing he said was that he had a weird story to tell me—so I told him I was into weird and he began.

He told me that a couple of years earlier he had attended a retreat that had changed his life. The retreat had been about the

work of a now-obscure psychiatrist named Fritz Kunkel. Kunkel had been a contemporary and colleague of Carl Jung and had worked on many of the same issues, especially individuation (Maslow's self-actualization). Kunkel had what was then a radical point of view: He believed that we couldn't reach this state of individuation unless there was a spiritual component, a willingness to look for higher meaning in our lives. Kunkel's work never really caught on back then, but Bart said that it had touched him deeply.

Bart went on to say that just a couple of weeks earlier Kunkel—whom he had never met—appeared in a dream. In the dream, Kunkel told Bart to tell the story of his work to Larry Wilson. That was the weird part for Bart—this kind of thing had never happened to him. He even checked it out with a couple of psychiatrist friends, who both told him to do what he was supposed to do: Get in touch with Larry Wilson.

Now Bart wanted me to get in touch with Abbot David, the Benedictine Brother who had led Bart's retreat. Completely hooked by this point, I said, "Great. Where does this guy live?" The final twist.

Bart, who thought I still lived in Minneapolis, said, "He lives in a little town you've never heard of called Pecos, New Mexico." Which, of course, was about ten miles from where I was sitting.

I don't mean to claim the spiritual high ground here, or to imply that I was somehow specially chosen. More truthful, I was at a point in my life where I was more open to the messages—the signs—that were always there.

My dream about the prince and his master/servant Ego was the first sign about Kunkel's work—about defeating ego-centeredness. Bart's dream was the second. Both, it turns out, had to do with Kunkel's message that life is a spiritual quest. Going as far you can with all that you have is ultimately about the deepest and most profound aspects of your life.

Bart came down on Good Friday and we visited Abbot David. Since then, Abbot David has been a teacher and counselor, helping us connect through Kunkel's work to that deep sense of meaning and that search for fulfillment that Viktor Frankl described.

For me, the outgrowth of this sequence of events has not been simply professional. Kunkel's work has been illuminating for me personally in my search to discover my true self and become whole.

In the early eighties, by most measures, I was at the top of my game. I had sold my company for a lot of money, I was in demand as a speaker, and I was highly respected in my field. Of course, I was also divorced twice and almost completely disconnected from my kids, who were going about their lives as if their father barely existed.

It wasn't as if I didn't have an explanation—I was a busy and successful guy, hard at work on that success dimension that Frankl described. Although I had to sacrifice time with my family now (so my ego's explanation went), they would eventually receive the financial benefits of my work when I died. And that would prove to them that I was a good dad.

I say this only because we are often exquisitely good at deceiving ourselves, at thinking that we are expressing our true selves when in fact it is our egos that are running the show. This is why ruthlessly telling the truth to ourselves is so important to playing to win: it's easy to deceive ourselves into thinking we are being true when we are not. As Kunkel wrote, "The ego is a cheat . . . but it is also a very clever one."

In retrospect, I know I was very focused on the prizes of playing not to lose. But as it happens, my choice was clearly becoming more painful—our divorce had deeply hurt the family, the wounds were open, and the family was unraveling. As for myself, as I got older, I was relieved that I had made it professionally, but there was always the gnawing sense of something missing.

Like a doctor who misdiagnoses an illness but serendipitously prescribes an appropriate course of action, I decided that I needed a change in everything. So I launched a business called Pecos River Learning and Conference Center in this unheard-of place called Pecos, New Mexico, which, incidentally, is in the middle of the Northern New Mexico culture that values family and family closeness as one of its highest priorities. But I wasn't aware of that at the time we broke ground.

Friends and associates thought I had completely lost my mind. And then as if to confirm my loss of common sense, I invited my kids to come down and launch the new business with me. It would be a family business—run by a family that at the time was wounded and barely speaking to one another. Well, at least not speaking much to me.

It should be emphasized that individuation is not a process we consciously decide on, but it is thrust upon us by our deepest instinct, the urge from within to become whole.

—Fritz Kunkel, *Selected Writings*

I had no idea what I was doing. My instincts told me that I needed to do something different. It just seemed like a good idea to go into business with my family; I could pass on some business experience and maybe launch them in new career directions. Of course, I was only slightly aware of the real reason, which is often what happens in the quest to discover who we are and why we are here. We are beset by an uneasy sense that things aren't right, yet we can't get to the bottom of it. We can't focus, we're bored, or we're depressed (we have dreams!).

For me, the deeper reason for going through the birthing pains of creating a company had much to do with healing and making myself whole. I had cut myself off from my family and now I had to become part of it again. In the process of creating, running, and, ultimately, selling Pecos River, we spent almost twelve years together—much of the time in the crisis mode of starting a new business. We fought, we cried, we negotiated, we went up an incredible learning curve together. It was like a crucible in which an intense heat transforms metals into something new. And now we are a family again. We are not remotely close to perfect, but had we not pulled together in those early years, we would've all spun off in our separate orbits and I would have been the worse off. I would not have known my grandchildren; I would not have helped heal the wounds of divorce. If I had not heeded that discomfort that sent me on my journey to become whole, I would have been successful, but I would have ended up divorced from my family.

The dilemma I found myself in is a very common one for many men and women. We get caught between the ego's desire for success and esteem and the no-less-insistent call for fulfillment and wholeness: balance, relationships, and meaning.

Which game are we playing? What is our life about? What do we tend to give up in order to play at the other table? I, predictably, gave up family for work. I felt more comfortable at work and I got my belonging and status needs met there.

Your choices may be utterly different. But these are the questions, this is the level of depth that we need to struggle with, in the journey to find ourselves—work, family, self-truth, pain, reconciliation, and personal growth. These are the paramount issues in growing up emotionally and growing up spiritually, and this is the area that we need to explore next.

SPIRITUAL BEINGS ON A HUMAN PATH

An important clarification. By *spiritual* we don't mean religious. We're not remotely qualified to write about those issues. By *spiritual* we mean exploring and giving credence to the spirit within—that sense of higher meaning that most of us eventually come in contact with. Certainly, that search often leads people to their Higher Power or to God. But for others it leads deeper into the primary and elemental necessities of life, and helps them answer the questions Why am I here? What is my life about? This is the spiritual adventure that we are interested in. Having said that, it seems that finding ourselves and finding a connection to a higher source are often simply different poems about the same experience.

> **T**he deepest and most profound process of human growth is individuation: becoming who God intended us to be.
>
> —Abbot David, Pecos Monastery

THE TRUE SELF

Kunkel taught that we each have a true self that is ours to discover. It is our spiritual being, here to serve, here to make a difference, here to express itself and help others. The great obstacle to discovering the true self is the ego-centered self. In Kunkel's work, the ego—the dragon—is what he calls the "false self," that sophisticated persona we project to the world that hides who we truly are.

We use the dichotomy of the false self (or the ego) and the true self not as a reflection of the way the brain is organized (there are no little

> **S**elf-actualization implies that there is a self to be actualized. A human being is not a tabula rasa, not a lump of clay. . . . He is something that is already there.
>
> —Abraham Maslow, The Farther Reaches of Human Nature

boxes in the brain labeled "ego" and "true self") but as a convenient way to label certain kinds of thinking and responding. When we are thinking and responding from that "map" that life is about "me," that is the ego-centered position. When we respond out of a belief that there is a larger picture and we are only a part of it, but that we have a unique role to play, that is the true self.

The False/True Dichotomy

FALSE SELF   **TRUE SELF**

Self-promotion   *Self-expression*
Self-protection   *Serve others*

WHO ARE YOU?

When you check in to a hospital or are taken there by ambulance, you get a visceral lesson in who you are. Your title and importance are stripped away and you get a plastic wristband instead. Your power suit is replaced by a robe that barely covers you and is exactly what all the other patients are wearing. You undergo endless, embarrassing, and often painful tests. Layer by layer, hospital personnel peel away the icons and trappings of your false self. In the hospital your history is gone, your salary and title are gone, your status is gone. You are stripped naked, lying on a steel table waiting for a procedure. You are no longer your job or title. You are the chest pain or the breast cancer in bed number four.

In the glare of the hospital lights, we come to realize that we are not our job, the car we drive, the house we live in, or the school we went to; all of that has been stripped away and now seems incredibly inconsequential. Who are you then? What is your life really about? These become the interesting questions.

THE PATH TO THE TRUE SELF: ME TO WE

Kunkel wrote that the path to the true self lies in the acceptance of and service to the larger "we." In a paradoxical way, the answers to our two key questions—Who am I? and Why am I here?—come not from looking inward, but from letting go of our ego-centeredness and allowing ourselves to become connected with and to serve a larger whole, to move from independence to interdependence. Human meaning exists not in "me" but in "we."

> **M**y deepest belief is that living as if you are dying sets us free.
>
> —Anne Lamott, *Bird by Bird*

A friend works for a medium-sized company by day and is a volunteer firefighter–emergency medical technician the rest of the time. He describes the difference between the ego and true self this way:

At work, it is a battle of jockeying for favor and promotions and protecting your interests—our egos are often caught up in the dynamics of an organization. I go home and the pager for the fire department goes off. We go to the scene and they usually aren't the dramatic moments you see on TV. It can be a kid hurt, an elderly man who is bedridden and has defecated on himself, the drunk who is a "frequent flyer" on the ambulance. When we are at our best—and we are not always—those moments are not ego-centered. They are focused on helping someone else and on easing pain and confu-

> **Y**es, there is a heaven. We create it every day when we protect a child, help an adult and revere our home, the earth.
>
> —George A. Erickson

sion. For me, those moments feel different—focused, outside of myself, wanting to help. During the moment—often in the midst of horror, death, and chaos—I feel as if I am making a difference and I am doing it with other people who are committed to the same purpose. It doesn't add stress to my life—although there are many very stressful moments and awful memories; it adds meaning. It gives me the opportunity to experience myself caring for others rather than obsessing about myself.

SPIRITUAL BUSINESS

Caring for others rather than obsessing about myself. Think about this in the very concrete world of business. Monday through Friday, we often make up that it is a battle out there to get what we want and to keep it from all other comers—other employees, managers, customers, suppliers. It is competition for seemingly scarce resources. The customer wants what is ours, employees want too much, and so on. People are out promoting and protecting themselves, projecting their false selves—titles, positions, jockeying for power and favor. The message is "Never show who you really are; you'll be eaten alive. Always take care of #1."

But Kunkel's work suggests a different game, that business might be more rewarding and fulfilling for individuals and organizations when it becomes more a reflection of our true selves than of our false selves. Rather than being ego-centered—how much money can we make, how can we "defeat" the competition or the customer?—it becomes a game of how we can help all those around us—our customers, our employees, our suppliers—get what they want.

As a result of helping others, we get what *we* want—and not just financially. It is in helping others and doing meaningful work for others that we can express our true selves, our spiritual nature, and get the sense of fulfillment that we often crave.

There is no reason why most businesses cannot move more in the direction of true service, instead of just lip service. It doesn't mean they can't be lean, tough, and competitive. But it does mean that they need to reflect on why they are in business in the first place: Is it simply to make money, to increase shareholder value at any cost to the other stakeholders in the business—customers, suppliers, employees, and the community? Or do they exist for a deeper, more compelling reason: to serve customers and solve their significant problems? It makes a difference which map you use.

The difference is manifested in a company's ability to recruit and hold on to committed, long-term employees. Organizations need individuals who work for more than just a paycheck, who are highly committed to solving significant problems and making a difference for customers. This isn't a training issue, this is a soul issue. What do you stand for? Why do you work? How do you serve?

The difference—in it for profit, or in it to solve problems and serve (and as a result make money)—is also manifested in an organization's ability to hold on to customers who continue to do business with you because they believe that you hold their interests before your interests.

Work and business—where we spend so much of our lives—can have a significant spiritual aspect, calling people to a higher purpose: to serve. Ironically, when corporations were first chartered by governments, that was their purpose: to serve the public. For example, when Chase Manhattan Bank was founded in New York in 1799 as the Manhattan Company, its purpose was not to lend money and perform other banking functions, but to supply treated water to a city swept by yellow fever.

Who we are at work is a reflection of our beliefs about ourselves, about others, and about which game we are playing. Are we about playing not to lose and that ego-centered self? Or are we about serving others, making the world a better place?

> **T**he empirical evidence for who you are and your life's purpose is in how you act.
>
> —John Allison, BB&T

Playing to win is ultimately about breaking through to higher meaning and service, both personally and professionally (it takes too much work to be schizophrenic: to be your true self at home and to self-promote and self-protect at work). Therein lies the path to emotional and spiritual maturity. How we do it is different for everyone, because each of us is a unique spiritual being, but we are linked by a common desire to have meaning and to serve.

UNFOLDING YOUR WINGS

That people all around you are beginning this journey is evident if you are paying attention. A forty-seven-year-old woman says, "It's time to unfold my wings." Another reports back—after opening her own bakery/gallery in a small town on the Pacific Coast—that it is the hardest thing that she has ever done in her life, but she wanted to try. Someone else describes her relentless pursuit for a college degree—inside an already-full life of work and kids. A thirty-year-old woman quits a lucrative job to be a social worker. A forty-five-year-old woman leaves her high-powered job to spend more

> **U**ntil I was about forty years old, I was afraid of my shadow. In the last few years many things have changed for me. I've come to realize that no matter who we are, we all have the same destination: death. I have chosen to live my life more consciously, more awake. I am trying to make fewer assumptions about myself, my family, and co-workers. Now, it is easier for me to enjoy everything I do at work and I am much more content with myself.
>
> —Rachel Rosen, British Airways

time with her kids. A thirty-five-year-old dad describes coaching Little League baseball as one of the top five experiences of his life. Another describes the passion he feels for his work, his customers, and the difference he is making. A fifty-one-year-old man beset with cancer goes home to the Catholic Church.

These examples represent simply a few weeks of listening to people describe their journeys to discover and live according to their true selves. In the grand scheme of things, they aren't dramatic stories. In the personal scheme of things, though, inside of each of those sentences is someone's adventure—into self-doubt, into fear—which began by asking in the middle of the night while staring out the window, "What is my life about?" In the personal scheme of things, these are all people on their hero's journey to find meaning and fulfillment. Something important pulls them away from their ego-centered desire to simply be comfortable and to take care of "me."

▼   ▼   ▼

After he retired, Carl Jung was asked how he had helped people get well. He said, "Most people came to me with an insurmountable problem. However, what happened was through our work together they discovered something more important than the problem and the problem lost its power and went away."

Discovering what allows our true selves to emerge is the secret to a magical life full of fulfillment and success. Serving others and expressing that service through our unique and important work is the secret.

> *I don't know what your destiny will be, but one thing I know: The only ones among you who will be really happy are those who will have sought and found how to serve.*
>
> —Kurt Hahn, Outward Bound

LOVING SERVICE

Letting go of our egocentric selves by serving others is the first step in finding our true selves. In caring for other human beings we discover ourselves and a joy that we cannot acquire when we are focused on self-promotion and self-protection.

Don Campbell, a senior facilitator for Pecos River, told us about the time in 1974 that he and his wife, Norma—both individuals "who are something more than people"—were assisting with the influx of Vietnamese children.

The children were being flown out of Saigon as the North Vietnamese invaded the city. Many of them came from orphanages scattered throughout South Vietnam. Others were children of diplomats who were fearful for their children's lives. Don and Norma's job was to meet the 747s that were carrying more than four hundred infants under the care of only three or four nuns. It is difficult to even imagine the chaos of all those babies and a few frantic nuns on a four-day country-hopping flight from Saigon. Many of the children arrived dirty, diseased, dehydrated, and malnourished. It was a bad, awful situation.

Don and Norma would take babies—many of whose eyes were stuck shut with infection and who hadn't had their diapers changed in four days—to bathe them, dress them, feed them, and generally get them ready for their next flight to various adoption organizations throughout the United States. Most tragically, during their long flight from Saigon, a few of the babies did not make it. Don remembers lifting the body of an apparently healthy baby boy out from beneath a seat. When he discovered the child was dead, he asked one of the nuns why the baby had died. She said, "This child came from one of the overcrowded orphanages. In the orphanages, there were so few of us. We just didn't have enough time to hold them

> **W**hat do we live for, if it is not to make life less difficult for each other?
>
> —George Eliot

and to love them. Very often these children would simply turn their heads to the wall and die."

There are many lessons here. The fundamental one is about love. We need it, crave it, can't live healthy lives without it. We require love in all its physical manifestations: touching, cuddling, hugging. And we require love in the nonphysical sense: knowing that someone cares for you and you care for him or her. Babies die—they often fail to thrive (what a tragically poignant turn of phrase)—without love. We too as adults "fail to thrive" without love and without the ability to love. Loving someone is the primordial experience of defeating our ego-centered selves and caring for another person.

Which is the main lesson of the story. The Campbells and those nuns were in loving service to those children. They came to the task with little regard for their ego-centered needs, but to help, to ease pain, to give love and take care of those infants whom they would never see again. It is a dramatic story—and Don and Norma Campbell are extraordinary people. Yet the fundamental gift we each have to give is what the Campbells gave, the gift of our love. It is not in short supply, it is not a scarce resource—we draw it from a very deep well. Of course, love exists on a spectrum, from simply caring about people, co-workers, employees, and customers to being deeply committed to spending your life with someone.

Loving service—whether for our customers, our friends, our significant others, or our children—requires of us the same four characteristics, but simply to different degrees: the empathic shift, understanding, acceptance, and involvement.

THE EMPATHIC SHIFT

The ego-centered self is incapable of mature love or of really caring for anyone other than "me." To care for someone and to love him or her, it is essential to be able to be other-centered, to shift our focus from ourselves to someone else. At Pecos River we call this the "empathic shift." Go back to the story of the man in the car honking to get your attention (Chapter 8). At first, most of us would have thought he was a jerk. Then when we learned that he had a child in the hospital (a new interpretation) most of us would have experienced an empathic shift: Now we cared about him and his problems more than our own.

The ability to make that kind of shift is the precursor to caring, serving, or loving another person. The requirement is the same whether it is love for the person to whom you have committed your life, or whether it is serving a customer or truly caring for a child you tutor twice a week.

UNDERSTANDING

Understanding is often the way we make the empathic shift. True understanding is the willingness to let go of our inaccurate, incomplete maps and interpretations and understand someone else's.

This is difficult (but not impossible). By way of example we have a simple exercise that we do in our classes. We pair people up based on their having fundamental disagreements (different inaccurate and incomplete maps) over "hot" topics—abortion, the church, the existence of God, the death penalty, and so on. In the exercise, the first person states his or her beliefs. The second person's task is only to understand the

> **T**here is no such thing as a weird human being. It's just that some people require more understanding than others.
>
> —Tom Robbins

first person's position. When the first person is finished, the test is to see whether the second person can demonstrate understanding by explaining what he or she heard. They might disagree, but they understand.

> **T**rue listening is a radical act, you risk being changed by it.
>
> —Juanita Brown, Whole Systems Associates

What this simple but difficult exercise demonstrates is that we normally don't listen and are rarely attempting to understand. We hear the word *abortion* and up pops our map called "Abortion" and also our map called "This is an argument and I need to be right and show the other person the errors in her thinking" (I need to self-promote). Instead of understanding the other person, more often we are engaged in judging—is he guilty of disagreeing with me?

Judging is the opposite of understanding. Make a "J" with your forefinger and thumb. Put it up against your forehead. The "J" stands for judgment and that is a symbol for how we walk around all day. When we are coming from our ego-centered selves, we are walking judges. What are our judgments based on? Our inaccurate, incomplete, and made-up maps.

Understanding asks you to let go of your interpretations and judgments and instead try to deeply understand another human being, a different group, an upset customer—or the single mom working in the low-paying, difficult service job who isn't serving you up to your expectations. Do you want to judge or do you want to understand? Which is more a reflection of who you truly are or want to be?

ACCEPTANCE

Truly and deeply understanding someone makes acceptance possible. *Acceptance* is the ability to embrace the differences, the frailties, the inconsistencies of others. It is a large and diverse world; we are each just a tiny piece of the puzzle; our maps of how things are are just small slivers of what is reality. We are one big family, but we each see the world differently. We ask our co-workers, friends, and family to accept us for who we are. In the same way, if we want to be in loving service to someone we need to accept them.

Does this mean that we need to accept everyone? No. For example, I may understand how abused children grow up to be abusers, but I do not have to accept their behavior—or even to accept them. But that is an extreme example. More commonly, we choose not to accept people for the tiniest of differences.

> **W**e are persistently, excruciatingly adept at many things that seem no more useful to modern life than the tracking of tides in the desert. At recognizing insider/outsider stature, for example, starting with white vs. black and grading straight into distinctions so fine as to baffle the bystander—Serb and Bosnian, Hutu and Tutsi, Crips and Bloods. We hold that children learn the discriminations from their parents, but they learn it fiercely and well, world without end. Recite it by rote like a multiplication table. Take it to heart, though it is neither helpful nor appropriate . . . a preference for the scent of our own clan: a thousand anachronisms dance down the strands of our DNA from a hidebound tribal past. . . . If we resent being bound by these ropes, the best hope is to seize them out like snakes, by the throat, look them in the eye and own up to their venom.
>
> —Barbara Kingsolver, *High Tide in Tucson*

From deep in our evolutionary past, when we couldn't trust the people we didn't know as family and clan, we have inherited a tendency that still has us see the world as essentially us versus them. We tend automatically to accept those who look like us, think like us, worship like us, dress like us, and so on, down to the finest detail, and we judge and reject those who are different, even when the differences are "so fine as to baffle the bystander."

To be in a loving and serving relationship we need to accept others—even though they are different, even though they don't think or believe as we do. When we accept as much diversity and difference as we can let in, then we become larger and we see a bigger picture than just what is fed us by our egos. Our egos crave the comfort and the scent of our own clan—which is a most limiting and inaccurate view of objective reality.

INVOLVEMENT

Loving service is about living and expressing our true selves through serving others. This is the wonderful paradox: We get what we want by helping others get what they want. We get feelings of fulfillment by serving others.

With that preface, the message that has been passed down though the ages is that it is the *involvement* that matters. We understand, we accept, and we get involved. Christ didn't say, "Gee, it would be a good idea to do something about those lepers. Here is my check for 20 drachmas." Christ went out and washed the feet of lepers. Siddhartha (Buddha) wrote, "I have found the other shore, now I help others across. I have found freedom, now I help others find freedom. I have found serenity, now I help others to become serene." The point is, we make a difference by getting involved.

A few years ago in one of our programs we heard this story.

A man in his mid-fifties described his family as fairly dysfunctional. He said that his parents—and especially his dad—had never really "parented" him. But he muddled through. When he was seven or eight, he tried out for a Little League team, even though his dad and mom had taught him nothing about baseball. When it came time for him to practice batting, he had no idea what to do. He picked up a bat, went up to the plate, and straddled it rather than standing next to it, to the great amusement of the other kids. What happened next altered the course of his life. The coach—no doubt some involved mom or dad—came up to him, held him lightly by the shoulders, and moved him to the proper position. The coach then said to him, in simple, simple words, "Here is where you need to stand. You'll do fine, you're going to be great."

At that moment this man knew what he wanted to do with his life: he wanted to be like that coach—involved—to help others figure out where to stand and to tell them that it would all work out and that they would be great.

Involvement is what changes lives. Involvement is spending time and energy to serve another person. Spending your time and energy is what lifts you out of yourself and allows you to experience the freedom and passion of being committed to something other than "me."

▼   ▼   ▼

Intention plus action equals results. Empathy, understanding, acceptance, and involvement—taking action—are what will propel us on our journey to our true selves.

CHAPTER

YOU ARE HERE TO DO IMPORTANT WORK

Our true self is best expressed when we are making a positive difference for others. Our ability to make a positive difference is best manifested when we are using the talents—the gifts—we have been given. Our highest calling is to express our true self by focusing our talents on the task of serving others.

THE TRUE SELF EXPRESSED

We each have a calling, a vocation, the work that is important for us to do. Ruth Kelly, of Santa Fe, New Mexico, worked at the original (and now held as the mythically creative) Bell Labs, raised five highly successful and happy kids, currently works for the governor of New Mexico, and is married to Paul Kelly, a Federal Circuit Court judge. Raising her kids, Ruth told them, "Find something to do that will interest you the rest of your life." She told them this over and over until they were no doubt sick of hearing it—but it sank in. Joseph Campbell, the great student and teacher of mythology, said it this way: "Follow your bliss." Different words, same message: Find the work that is important for you to do.

> *S*elf-actualized people are devoted to working at something which is very precious to them—a calling or vocation in the old sense. They are working at something which fate has called them to somehow and which they love, so that the work-joy dichotomy in them disappears.
>
> —Abraham Maslow, *The Farther Reaches of Human Nature*

USE YOUR TALENT!

If you want joy from your work, find work that uses your talents. A number of years ago I spent a week with John Crystal, who at that time was helping people as a life and career planner. (John's first career—talk about doing something interesting—was as a member of the OSS, the precursor to the CIA in World War II.) One of the first things that John did was sketch out this matrix:

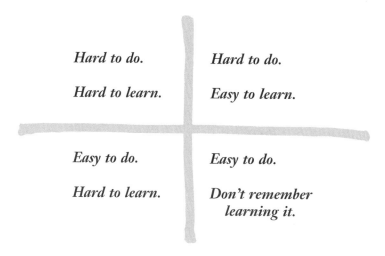

Hard to do.

Hard to learn.

Hard to do.

Easy to learn.

Easy to do.

Hard to learn.

Easy to do.

Don't remember learning it.

He then asked this question: "Which of the four does our society most value?" Remembering all those years of character-building Latin classes in Catholic school, I piped up, "Hard to do and hard to learn." He agreed and then asked, "Do you know what 'easy to do, don't remember learning it' is?" I must have looked confused because he shouted at me, "It's your talent! And the problem is that most people don't value their talent because it wasn't hard to learn or hard to do. Yet, talent is what God gave us to make the world a better place."

Talent is a gift we have been given. We each have talent—the easy-to-do, don't-remember-learning-it part of who we are. Talent calls us: The writer wakes up and writes, the painter paints, the entrepreneur can't help but start something new—it is what is natural and easy for us to do. Each of us is capable of finding our talent and bringing it to life.

But there are often a lot of "shoulds" and "thou shalts" that get in the way. You should be what your parents want you to be, you should be what you think is appropriate for you to be. "Thou shalt be a _____ (fill in the blank)." The spiritual journey, though, takes you to your true self—not your parents' or society's map of who you are. Our talent—which most of us can taste, feel, and sense—is the neon sign pointing in the right direction. Discover your talent, use it, and you will find the way to your true self.

IMPORTANT WORK

But discovering and developing your talent isn't enough; it needs to be harnessed to important work. John Allison, whom we've quoted a number of times, is chairman and CEO of BB&T, a North Carolina–based regional bank. BB&T has grown from $600 million in assets in 1980 to $28 billion today, but in the late seventies, it was a sleepy little North Carolina bank and John was a young officer in the bank—and not a happy one. One day at lunch, he discovered that a number of his peers felt the same way. Over that lunch they all came to the same decision: to resign and seek their work and fortunes elsewhere.

That afternoon, four of them walked into the CEO's office and very cordially announced their decision. They said, in essence, this is a nice bank, but it's not where we want to spend the rest of our careers. The CEO, in a moment of mature wisdom, didn't get upset, but instead asked, "What would it take for you to stay?" The group went through a laundry list of things that had to be changed if they were to stay, from the composition of the management team to changing the strategic direction of the organization to spending more money on training people to opening new markets. The CEO pondered the list for a moment and then said, "If those are the things you want, go do them."

And so their adventure began. Doors opened, bridges appeared. They took this sleepy little bank and turned it into a purpose-driven, customer-focused regional powerhouse. It wasn't enough to have a job, to use their talents. They wanted to be doing important work—and they were willing risk their careers to make it happen. Reflecting back on the experience, John says, "We are inspired by important work. If we are not doing something which is important to us, then we need to change what we are doing, because we need a personal sense of purpose."

USING YOUR TALENTS TO DO IMPORTANT WORK

It's up to you to define what is important work for you. But go back to Dick Leider's seniors. In looking back, they said they wanted to have left a legacy, to have made a positive difference. That is a good definition of important work: work that will make a positive difference, work that will make the world a better place.

	Doesn't Use My Talent	**Uses My Talent**
Important	*Interesting*	*Passion!*
Not Important	*Deadly dull!*	*I can do this in my sleep!*

The goal is to be doing that kind of work using your talent. That is how we find passion, purpose, and meaning. We become—to some extent—our work, our work becomes us. It doesn't mean that you are your job; jobs come and go. But your work, your purpose, endures. It doesn't mean that you're a workaholic. Your work is what inspires you, gets you up in the morning, makes you feel alive and contributing. It means that you have tapped into the well of your talent and are using it to solve significant problems.

DO WHAT YOU LOVE OR LOVE WHAT YOU DO

Here is the imperative. The mission is to find and live your true self, to do important work using your talents to serve others. This is difficult to do when you find yourself in the "deadly dull" box or the "I'm asleep" box.

So what are your options? First, you can change what you are doing—quit your job, find new work, go to school, try something new, take the risk of writing a novel, sculpting, selling, inventing . . . whatever. Get yourself by hook or by crook into the passion box, doing important work that uses your talents.

But often we jump to something new—in the hopes of finding fulfillment—and we miss the opportunity in front of us. Your second option is to discover or rediscover how to serve, how to bring meaning to what you currently do.

This second option is often the more realistic choice. In front of our noses are usually dozens of ways

> **W**ork is love made visible. And if you cannot work with love but only with distaste, it is better that you should leave your work and sit at the gate of the temple and take alms of those who work with joy.
>
> —Kahlil Gibran

that we can bring service and meaning to our lives and work. If you are a manager, how can you better serve your employees? If you're a salesperson, how can you better serve your customers—and help them get what they want? If you're an employee, how can you better serve and add meaning to the employees around you? How can you make work and life better for them? How can you better serve and help your family find its way?

Most often, finding your passion doesn't require you to join the Peace Corps. It requires you to reexamine your current situation and see the opportunities to serve and add meaning that are right before your eyes. It is never an easy, convenient path. In this kind of journey, sometimes the apple cart will be upset, sometimes you'll upset your parents, your family, your friends (and surely scare yourself!), but this is your hero's journey. There will be problems (eighty-three of them), there will be setbacks, but you will grow. If you persevere, then you have a shot at joy, passion, and fulfillment.

FEAR NOT

"Fear not" is easy to write, sometimes hard to put into motion—most commonly because of fear itself. It is the ego in us that fears being lost if the true self is allowed to express itself and serve others rather than taking care of and basking in the glory of "me." It is largely the ego that fears the possible discomfort that comes with, for example, quitting a cushy job in order to find work or a calling that inspires you.

A friend relates this story.

> *I was seventeen and struggling with whether or not I believed in God. I had compiled a list of the pros and cons about whether or not I should join a church—any church. At that time, I chose not to join and I prided myself on making an intellectually valid decision. Thirty years later, in retrospect, I understood that the true*

reason that I chose not to believe was that I was afraid that I would lose control of myself—that this higher calling was so powerful that it would alter me forever. In other words, my ego was afraid of being diminished in the service to a higher cause.

Fear of change is often that ego-centered self holding on to what it knows, holding tight to its childlike belief that it is the center of the universe.

So when you ask, "Who am I and why am I here?" the ego often steps in right at that moment. You find yourself thinking, "Whoa, let's not ask for something that puts me in a position of failing, being wrong, being rejected, or being emotionally uncomfortable. Let's not ask for something that would challenge the supremacy of 'me.'" For many, the game stops right there.

Ignore that voice! In doing so, you will find that you have been blessed with the transcendent gift to think, to Stop, Challenge, and Choose: "What do I really want? What is my life truly about? What do I have to fear?" Finally, you will find that you have the creativity to choose your path, to find your own way.

▼ ▼ ▼

This path has been illuminated and taught down through the ages. The message has been that we have nothing to fear but fear itself. The message has been to go forth, have courage, fear not. Above all, heed those words—have courage, fear not. Let them sink inside you, absorb them, give them personal meaning. In doing so, they will illuminate the path to your true self.

In our lives we often stand on the edge of the miraculous. We stand at the very edge of becoming larger, of becoming who we are destined to be. But those moments are always accompanied by fear—it is the price we pay for fulfilling our potential. If there is not fear, then we're not on the edge; we're not pushing the limits of our comfort zones.

It is like Olympic athletes—the skaters, the gymnasts, the ski racers—who always seem to be falling; it is because they are on the very edge of their technical and emotional abilities. They risk failure to discover who they truly can become. For the rest of us, being on the edge means fear and anxiety. But what it is that we fear exactly? Are we so afraid of failure that we back away from growth? Are we so afraid of being rejected that we choose to play it safe and comfortable? Are we so afraid of thinking on our own that we choose to safely follow conventional wisdom?

What exactly is there to fear? The spiritual power of the phrase "fear not" is for those moments. The message is that there is nothing in those moments to truly fear—if we stop, challenge, and think, if we focus on what it means to be our true selves. "Fear not" comes from this most powerful, spiritual part of us. It is there when we need it; we simply need to listen.

PART VII

▼▼▼

In *The Adventures of Alice in Wonderland,* Alice came up to the caterpillar and asked him which road she should take. He asked where she was going. She replied that she didn't know. He said, "Then it doesn't matter what road you take."

PART VIII

Choosing Growth

If you've gotten this far

in *Play to Win!* the logical question is "So now what?" What are you going to do next? In this part, we want to help you answer that question. But be forewarned, it might require you to choose to do something different in order to get different results. You might have to utter one of the most powerful phrases in the English language: "I choose." "Choose" is the incantation of desire, decision, and action. When we say "I choose," we commit to a course of action and we eliminate alternatives. When we say "I choose," doors open and bridges appear.

So stop—right now, at this moment—and ask yourself this: Do I want to play to win and discover how to live more deeply out of my true self? If I do, what am I going to *choose* to do about it?

We wrote earlier that intention plus action creates results. When we choose, we take action, we do something different—

starting with changing our think-ing—in order to get different results.

Intention + action = results

People often say they want to change—they want more mean-ingful work or better relation-ships. But then we ask ques-tions—What is your plan? What are you going to do differently tomorrow to change your results?—and this commonly brings people up short. Such questions startle us because we have intention, but no plan to take action, no idea of how to get to the results we want.

In this last part of *Play to Win!* we are going to help you put intention into action. We are going to help you create a plan to change.

What we are going to work on next is based on Stop, Challenge, and Choose. To create a plan—any plan for change—

you first need to *stop:* get off the freeway of life for a while, reflect on who you are and who you want to be, and create a plan to get you there. Next, you need a plan to *challenge* and overcome the obstacles to your plan—including the internally gen-erated obstacles, the often irra-tional fears our egos create to maintain the status quo. Finally, you *choose* to be committed to change, committed to going down a new path.

There are many levels of commitment, from passive inter-est to absolute commitment. It is important to tell the truth to yourself about your level of com-mitment to any plan you create for yourself.

Clearly, individuals who have a high level of commitment are much more likely to succeed. It is important, then, to create a plan that is realistic, but inspires your commitment at the highest level.

An important note: Power and clarity in this kind of work come from taking your time, and writing your plan down. In his

LEVELS OF COMMITMENT:

▼ **Level 1: Passive interest**
We offer no resistance to the idea or the desired results, but we are unwilling actually to change.

▼ **Level 2: Active interest**
We find value in the plan, it sounds sensible and agreeable. But we don't initiate actions that would start us down the path. (We'll wait until the dragon gets to us!)

▼ **Level 3: Compliance**
We do what is asked, but we don't have the commitment or energy to motivate ourselves.

▼ **Level 4: Qualified commitment**
We are positive and focused on the plan. We willingly move forward, but we may be overwhelmed by obstacles leading to slow progress or a complete stop. We are committed, but not at a sufficient level to overcome the problems and obstacles.

▼ **Level 5: Absolute commitment**
At this level, we will do whatever is needed to create the desired results. We will use creativity, courage, and persistence to deal with problems and obstacles.

work as a career planner, Dick Leider has observed that most people spend more time and work planning their vacations than they do their lives.

So take your time. Take time to think. To Stop, Challenge, and Choose. Write your plan down and keep it with you.

SIX STEPS TO AN OPTIMAL FUTURE

This is a chapter of questions—
six questions to help you create a plan for change, one that you can
be committed to at Level 5. You will
need paper and pen or pencil (or a

THE SIX STEPS:

1. **Identify your values.**

2. **Identify your talents.**

3. **Create the action statement of your true self—your purpose.**

4. **Develop your personal vision.**

5. **Create your plan.**

6. **Identify obstacles and support.**

computer) to complete the exercise. The final draft can be used as a permanent record (in your day planner or on your computer).

Good plans—whether for individuals or organizations—begin from the inside out: What are your values? What are your core maps? You then move outward toward talents and purpose and, finally, you create a plan.

STEP #1: IDENTIFY YOUR VALUES

In the world of the Plains Indians, when a leader or young warrior believed in something deeply and was passionately committed, he tied himself to stakes in front of an approaching enemy to symbolize the depth and passion of his beliefs. He staked himself to make a statement for all to see. We each have values that we hold deeply and passionately enough to "stake ourselves out" for.

Values are those ideals, principles, and morals that shape our core maps, our view of how the world seems to work, which in turn create our priorities and the choices and decisions we make. We've provided a short list of values to stimulate your thinking.

Example values:

Accountability	Fairness	Independence
Authenticity	Family	Integrity
Beauty	Fun	Loyalty
Comfort	Growth	Openness
Competitiveness	Happiness	Peace
Cooperation	Health	Spirituality
Courage	Honesty	Trust

Question: What are my top ten values?

List your values in priority order and try to eliminate the values that conflict. For example, "An eye for an eye" and "Turn the other cheek" are values in conflict (as are cooperate and compete, under some conditions). If you have values in conflict, you need to either pick one or prioritize them in order to have your values truly be helpful.

STEP #2: IDENTIFY YOUR TALENTS

Talents are the physical and mental strengths that we have been gifted with and are good at (things that are easy to do, that we don't remember learning). We were either born with them or developed them so well that they come naturally and easily. Our talents are what we are drawn to do—the writer wakes up and writes, the mathematician thinks in equations, the empathic person thinks about people.

Example talents:

Academic	Empathic
Articulate	Good judge of people
Artistic	Good listener
Athletic	Good speaker
Courageous	Good with numbers
Creative	Good with words
Detail oriented	Mechanically adept
Disciplined	Supportive

Question: What are my talents?

STEP #3: CREATE THE ACTION STATEMENT OF YOUR TRUE SELF

Your *purpose* is the action statement of your true self—that part of you that is larger than your egocentric self and that is committed to making a positive difference by doing important work using your talents. Your purpose defines what your life is all about. It is enduring and, like the true self, it is not dependent on a job or circumstances—it is about your life. A purpose statement can be amended and changed—but only rarely, because it is an expression of the deepest part of you.

Compelling purpose statements are succinct. We can memorize them and use them to bring us back on track. An event occurs. Stop, Challenge, and ask this question: "Is my response consistent with my purpose in life?" This will help you make choices and decisions consistent with who you are and who you want to be.

> **THE PECOS RIVER PURPOSE:**
>
> **We are committed to helping individuals and organizations everywhere rediscover their courage and creativity and use them in the service of creating a better world.**

Example purpose statements:

▼ I serve others through my work, actions, and words.
▼ I continuously learn and grow in order to succeed in everything I do and make the world a better place.
▼ I use my talents as a communicator to help people better understand each other.

Characteristics of an effective purpose statement:

▼ Concise and clear—no more than three simple sentences
▼ Present tense

▼ Simple to understand and remember
▼ Congruent with your values and uses your talents
▼ Includes whom or what you are in service to
▼ Can be accomplished and lived by your effort alone
▼ Inspires you!

Question: What is my purpose?

Write a few drafts of your purpose statement (following the guidelines listed above) and then write a final draft.

STEP #4: DEVELOP YOUR PERSONAL VISION

Values, talents, and your purpose—the action statement of your true self—define who you are. It is from that core that you can then begin to develop a plan. First, though, you have to create a vision of how you want your plan to turn out.

A powerful and compelling vision gives us a reference point in the future from which to make decisions instead of driving through life looking in the rearview mirror. A vision allows you to make key decisions based on whether or not they are consistent with where you want to go. A personal vision statement expresses your dream of how you want things to be, how you want it all to turn out. As the caterpillar admonished Alice, you have to know where you're going in order to get there.

A personal vision statement answers two questions: What will I be doing? and What will it feel like?

Characteristics of an effective vision statement:

▼ Defines a specific point in time, one to two years in the future, for example

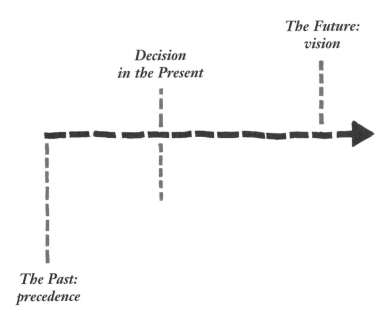

- ▼ Present tense

- ▼ Short and compelling sentences

- ▼ Congruent with your values, talents, and purpose

- ▼ Includes all aspects of your life: personal, professional, family, mental, emotional, and spiritual

- ▼ Inspires you!

Example vision statements:

- ▼ It's *x* years from now, and I am a manager in my department, and I feel competent and respected.

- ▼ It's *x* years from now, and I am more assertive and truthful in meetings, and I feel a high sense of integrity.

▼ I am spending weekends with my family.

▼ I am taking more risks.

Question: What is my personal vision?

STEP #5: CREATE YOUR PLAN

A compelling vision statement is but a single step toward creating your future. The next step is to figure out how you are going to bridge the gap between where you are and where you want to go.

Strategies

The first part of the plan is to create *strategies*, the broad initiatives that set out the general direction of the plan without a lot of detail. "I will go back to school for two years to finish my degree" is a broad strategy. It describes what you are going to do but it doesn't give the details. We recommend that you create and write a maximum of four strategies in order to keep the process manageable. Keep the strategies concise and direct—one idea per strategy statement.

Question: Which four strategies will help me get to my vision?

Tactics

Each strategy needs to be broken down into *tactics*. Tactics define the basics: the who, what, when, and where. For example, if your strategy is "I will go back to school for two years to finish my degree," the tactics would tell details like when you will start, what school you'll attend, how you will pay for it, and so on, down to who will watch the kids while you study.

Question: For each of my strategies, what are the important tactics—that is, the who? what? when? how?

STEP #6: IDENTIFY OBSTACLES AND SUPPORT

Winston Churchill wrote that plans are worthless but planning is indispensable. The reason that plans fail is that in the real world there are unpredictable and unavoidable obstacles and problems. The day we put our plan into action, something will have changed that will require us to amend the plan.

Rather than naively starting down the road, we need to think about potential obstacles and have a plan to deal with them. Here is an exercise to help: Imagine that it is one year from now. You've achieved your vision. Think of the obstacles you encountered and how you overcame them to get to where you are now.

Question: What obstacles do I foresee and how will I overcome them?

To achieve your vision you will require support to overcome obstacles and to keep you motivated. Imagine again that it is one year from now. You've achieved your vision. What kind of support did you need? What person(s) would win the "best supporting actor" for helping you achieve your vision?

Question: What support from what people do I foresee I will need, and how will I ask for it?

NOW THAT YOU HAVE A PLAN . . .

Refine it

We suggest that now you refine your plan so that it is simple but comprehensive and the language inspires you! Put it away for a day or so and then come back and read it. If it still makes sense and motivates you to Level 5 commitment, it's ready. Put it in your day planner or on your computer where you'll see it daily.

Share it

It is powerful to go public with your plan. Yes, we put pressure on ourselves to accomplish what we've said. But when we go public, doors open and bridges appear—help arrives. Support comes out of the woodwork. To formalize this, we recommend that you ask someone to be your "developmental buddy," to support you along your developmental path. This is someone to bounce ideas off of, someone who will support you and hold up a mirror. Preferably this person is also going through a change and growth process so that you can support your buddy in return.

WHAT TO DO WITH YOUR PLAN:

▼ **Refine it**

▼ **Share it**

▼ **Use it**

▼ **Stop, Challenge, and Choose**

Use it

The plan is worthless unless you use it. Start today. Remember the old story from the motivational-tapes era of the businessman who was the king of self-affirmation? He'd get up in the morning and listen to motivational tapes in the shower. He had his mirror plastered with slogans and positive affirmations. He'd look in the mirror and say to himself, "You can do it!" He was the most motivated, well-intentioned guy on earth—but he never left his house.

You need to leave the house! Start with small steps. Win small victories first. But begin. Hermann Hesse wrote, "In all beginnings dwells a magic force for guarding us and helping us to live." Start today.

Stop, Challenge, and Choose

Finally, remember that Stop, Challenge, and Choose is the fundamental skill to use to stay on plan. When you do not feel positive (or at least neutral) about where you are going or you are being pulled backwards, *stop* and ask yourself: Is this choice, is this feeling, helping me or hurting me in my pursuit toward a goal or action plan? *Challenge* your irrational thinking. *Choose* to stay on course.

Persistence is no doubt one of the most valuable attributes in making progress toward a goal. Stop, Challenge, and Choose is a tool of persistence. It is best used to intervene as we lose focus on our plan or to help us assure that one of our eighty-three problems doesn't become a barrier that is impossible to cross.

▼   ▼   ▼

A strategy to change. The powerful incantation "I choose." A commitment to do whatever it takes. Under the laws of life in our universe, this is how we create the highest probability of creating the results we want. It might be difficult, but it is rarely impossible. Don't let difficulty stop you, because it is from doing difficult things that we truly grow. It is from doing difficult things that we call out our ability to play to win.

DEEPLY PREPARED PEOPLE CREATE THEIR OWN WEATHER

A few years ago I went on a four-day adventure in the High Country wilderness of the Sangre de Cristo Mountains north of Santa Fe. We were divided into essentially two types of people. There were the "outdoor" enthusiasts who exulted in being in the mountains, and then there were the rest of us—grumpy city dwellers. As soon as we hit the trail and began moving up into forest, the city dwellers were hit by the realization that it was going to be uncomfortable—cold, rainy, and wild. In front of us were the Truchas peaks, which we intended to climb. It had sounded like a great idea a month ago, but now they were shrouded in clouds and the rumble of thunder. They looked foreboding and unapproachable. We asked ourselves, "Why are we doing this? It's going to be uncomfortable and even dangerous— why don't we just turn back now and admit defeat?"

But encouraged and kept in good spirits by the outdoor folks, up we marched, farther and farther from the comforts of home. We arrived at our camp—a meadow under the sheer pitches of the Truchas Mountains. It was stunning . . . but our "home" was four makeshift tarps.

We soon discovered that in the mountains the weather rules and it is completely unpredictable. In our four days, it rained, snowed, hailed, we had winds that blew out the tarps . . . and we had a couple hours of sun.

> **L**ife shrinks or expands in proportion to one's courage.
>
> —Anaïs Nin

Beyond the unpredictability of the weather—now it was sunny, boom, then it was hailing—were the reactions of the people. The city folks, myself included, got mad and complained loudly and bitterly about the event of the weather—the damp, the cold, and the "Oh, my God, it's snowing!" We had expected sunny weather, darn it! And we were mad that it wasn't happening! We eventually found a bottle of tequila and retired to the driest tarp to commiserate.

The outdoors folks were quite different. When it rained, they put on ponchos; when it got cold and snowed, they put on more layers. When the sun came out, they stripped down to T-shirts and shorts and enjoyed the warmth on their bodies. The difference was that they were prepared, by training and experience, for anything.

What hit me was this: There is no such thing as bad weather, just unprepared people. The weather just happens; it is neither bad nor good, cruel nor pleasant; it just is. We interpret it as bad or good because of how it affects us, but in reality, weather is just weather. All we can really do is be prepared.

On our little wilderness adventure, the prepared people handled the weather with much more calm and creativity than the rest of us did. They were ready for almost anything. They didn't remain upset when all of a sudden the tarps blew over; they solved the problem and got on with it. It was all an adventure to them. What would they learn this time? How far would their limits be pushed? What would they see? What would they experience?

And that is the clue. In the adventure of our lives, good things happen, bad things happen, and—boom—terrible things happen. In our lives we will each face choices that will determine who we will become. We will all face the crises of living: pain, loss, death. The individuals with the best probability of responding with courage and creativity are those who are best prepared emotionally and spiritually. Prepared people can handle all kinds of weather; deeply prepared people see the weather as a challenge and as an opportunity to grow.

With work and thinking, we too can become deeply prepared for the rest of our lives. We can become so thoroughly prepared that we begin to positively influence what happens to us; we begin to create our own weather.

Think about it. Once we understand that we are here for a reason—that we are spiritual beings on a human path—then we can start making choices that lead us deeper and deeper into our true selves. We strike out on our own, we make those courageous choices that lead us in directions that we would never before have taken had we settled for just playing not to lose all our lives. As a result, we create our own weather.

When we understand that there is much less to avoid, much less to fear, when we see life as an opportunity to grow, we attempt more, we face more challenges, and we grow. As a result, we get emotionally and spiritually stronger and more like those experienced outdoors folks: prepared for almost anything, exulting in our lives, and creating our own weather.

STOP, CHALLENGE, AND CHOOSE

The linchpin in all of this is Stop, Challenge, and Choose. It is because life comes at us so fast and point blank that Stop, Challenge, and Choose is such an important skill. It is vital to know what results we want. It is crucial to discover our true selves. Equally important is the ability at any moment to Stop, Challenge, and Choose: What is happening? How am I interpreting what is happening? How do I want it to turn out? It is this simple skill—that needs to become as natural as breathing—that is the life vest. It will save us when the world seems crazed and irrational and we feel tugged by "negative" feelings and the tiny irritants that threaten to distract us daily.

In Part I we quoted Bertrand Russell: "Most people would rather die than think; many do." The simplest message of this book is to think, to use our brains to live and make important choices consciously and to be persistent in the pursuit of the answers to those two most important questions—Why am I here? What is my life about? Stop, Challenge, and

> **W**e cannot put off living until we are ready. The most salient characteristic of life is its coerciveness; it is always urgent, here and now, without any possible postponement. Life is fired at us point blank.
>
> —José Ortega y Gasset

Choose is the tool to accomplish both—to help you think deeply and clearly.

THE PARADOX OF TIME

> **T**o the old man planting trees: "You live as if you will live forever, I as if I will die tomorrow. Which one of us is right?"
>
> —*Zorba the Greek*

The frame for all of this, of course, is time and the number of heart-beats you have left.

And time is a paradox. On one hand, you may live well into your nineties. The question then becomes what you're going to do with all that time. How are you going to live fully and express yourself? Are you going to continue to get the same results you've always gotten, think the same thoughts, do the same things for twenty, forty, sixty more years? Or are you going to launch out in new directions, take risks, try something totally different? Will you look back and say, "I made something of my life, I made a difference."

On the other hand, you are at risk of perishing tomorrow. In that case, the question becomes how you're living your life right now. Are you avoiding situations that are important to your growth? Are you making stuff up that is harming you? Are you living so much in the past or so far in the future that you're missing the simple pleasure of being alive? Are there people who need your forgiveness and whom you need to forgive? Are there people *now* who need your love and whom you need to love?

Time is the master complicator, because you don't know which scenario will be yours. To live dedicated to objective reality, you need to make your choices in ways that honor both possibilities: a long life or one cut short. Each important choice you make needs to reflect the paradox of time. By important choices, we don't just mean choices about what the rest of your life should be. We also mean choices about whether you need to carry anger for some person, or is it more important to choose to understand and forgive? Is it more important to worry about next year's plan and budget, or to choose to hold tight to the hand clutching yours and be in the world of a six-year-old?

Events, choices, consequences. In this trinity that makes up our lives, it is our choices that tell us who we are, what our lives are about, and how we are using the time we have left.

THE POWER OF CHOICE

Which brings us back to Viktor Frankl and his final freedom: We have the freedom and power to choose the way we respond to whatever life hands us. We have the freedom and accountability to make choices. Frankl saw his own life as a testament to this freedom. His career as a psychotherapist and neurologist was interrupted by the Second World War and the Holocaust. He spent three years in four Nazi camps: Theresienstadt, Auschwitz, Kaufering III, and Türkheim. He lost his wife, Tilly, and his father, mother, and brother in the camps.

In *Man's Search for Meaning* Frankl wrote:

> *We who lived in concentration camps can remember the men who walked through the hut comforting others, giving away their last piece of bread. They may have been few in number, but they offered sufficient proof that everything can be taken from a man but one thing: the last of the human freedoms—to choose one's attitude in any given set of circumstances, to choose one's own way. And there were always choices to make. Every day, every hour, offered the opportunity to make a decision, a decision which determined whether you would or would not submit to those powers which threatened to rob you of your very self, your inner freedom;*

which determined whether or not you will *become the plaything of circumstance, renouncing freedom and dignity to become molded into the form of the typical inmate.*

God willing, none of us will face a Holocaust. None of us tomorrow will face Sophie's choice, having our children torn from us, one selected for the showers, one for the labor camps. Tomorrow, the vast majority of us will have normal days: We will go to work, go to school, stay home. We will all face inconveniences—from losing a job to the anger of a boss to the acting out of a child. And yes, we will also face personal tragedies. At each of those moments, there will be choices to be made. Each of those choices will define who we are and what we stand for.

Yes, it takes courage to respond like the few who gave away their last pieces of bread. Yes, it takes courage to respond—no matter what the weather or the obstacles—in ways that reflect your true self. Yes, it takes courage and creativity to live your life committed to making a difference. But you have the courage, you have the creativity. Playing to win is about rediscovering them and using them to create a better world, even if it is the small world of your family, friends, and work. We are here to help each other on our journeys, we are here to make a difference.

Go forth, fear not.

"Larry's Poem"

I face my dragons everyday
I find the courage to chase them away.
I stop, I breathe, I center, I observe;
I challenge my thinking when it's absurd.

I choose the thoughts that are best for me,
And those that are closest to reality.

I find the spirit that is truly me
And serve the world to set it free.

I don't have to do what I've always been
I learn and grow and that's how I win.

—*Larry Wilson, 2004*

Notes

59   We've adapted this model: For advanced work in this model, see Greenberger and Padesky, *Mind over Mood.*

64   What the research demonstrated: "Prisoners of Silence."

74   As a result of this extensive work: O'Toole, *Leading Change.*

112   From our experience and the research: Especially the work of Dr. Albert Ellis.

127   . . . she outsmarted the Sicilian: Goldman, *The Princess Bride.*

140   He went so far as to say: Dalton, *The Deming Management Method.*

161   Up to George comes the critic: Sondheim, "Sunday in the Park," n.p.

188   Ironically, when corporations were first chartered: Estes, *Tyranny of the Bottom Line.*

189   . . . when Chase Manhattan: Uchitelle and Kleinfeild, "The Downsizing of America."

230   He lost his wife: Frankl, *Recollections: An Autobiography.*

230   We who lived in concentration camps: Frankl, *Man's Search for Meaning*, p. 86.

Sources

Interviews by Hersch Wilson

John Allison, chairman and CEO, BB&T Corporation, Winston-Salem, N.C.

Juanita Brown, president, Whole Systems Associates, Mill Valley, Calif.

Linda Brown, senior facilitator, Pecos River Change Management, Honolulu

Tracy Burke, M.S.W., Santa Fe

Don Campbell, senior facilitator, Pecos River Change Management, San Diego

Thomas G. Cigarran, chairman, president, and CEO, American HealthCorp, Nashville

Dan Dean, formerly with Aon Consulting, Phoenix

Sarah DiGiorgio, British Airways, Brooklyn

Tim Flanagan, general agent, Mass Mutual, Bala Cynwyd, Pa.

Jamie Gagan, M.D., St. Vincent's Hospital, Santa Fe

John Griffin, secretary of natural resources, State of Maryland, Annapolis

Jim Kearns, former executive vice president, DuPont Fibers, Wilmington, Del.

Ruth Kelly, director of boards and commissions, State of New Mexico, Santa Fe

Rob Knapp, first vice president, Midwest district director, Merrill Lynch, Carmel, Ind.

John Marshall, manager of human resource management, Dofasco Steel, Hamilton, Ont., Canada

Maxie C. Maultsby, Jr., M.D., professor of psychiatry, Howard University Hospital, Washington, D.C.

Helen Mills, senior vice president, Aon Consulting, Washington, D.C.
Dale Moss, executive vice president, British Airways, Brooklyn
Edwin Peterson, vice president of sales, Martin Engineering,
　　　Neponset, Ill.
Bob Root, partner, ORION Learning, San Diego
Rachel Rosen, British Airways, Brooklyn
Paul Ruane, director of sales training, Schering-Plough HealthCare,
　　　Liberty Corner, N.J.
Wendy Steele, partner, ORION Learning, San Diego
John Walker, president and CEO, Interface Ltd., Berkhamsted,
　　　Herts., U.K.
Gordon Whitener, president and CEO, Interface Americas, Inc.,
　　　Cartersville, Ga.
Billy Weisman, president and CEO, Weisman Enterprises, Minneapolis

Interviews from Wilson and Wilson: *Changing the Game*

Alan Braslow, formerly with Five Technologies, Woodcliff, N.J.
Eric Carlson, Du Pont Automotive Development Center, Troy, Mich.
Kathy Monthei, formerly with Delta Dental Plan of California, Oakland

Books, Articles, Other Published Sources

Argyris, Chris. *Overcoming Organizational Defenses: Facilitating
　　　Organizational Learning.* Needham Heights, Mass.: Allyn & Bacon,
　　　1990.
———. "Teaching Smart People How to Learn." *Harvard Business
　　　Review* (March–April 1991).
Castañeda, Carlos. *The Teachings of Don Juan: A Yaqui Way of Knowledge.*
　　　Berkeley and Los Angeles: University of California Press, 1968.
Dalton, Mary. *The Deming Management Method.* New York: Dodd Mead,
　　　1986.
Ellis, Albert. *The Practice of Rational Emotive Therapy (RET).* New York:
　　　Springer, 1987.
Estes, Ralph W. *The Tyranny of the Bottom Line: Why Corporations Make
　　　Good People Do Bad Things.* San Francisco: Berrett-Koehler, 1996.

Frankl, Viktor. *Man's Search for Meaning: An Introduction to Logotherapy.*
    3rd ed. New York: Simon & Schuster, 1984.

————. *Viktor Frankl Recollections: An Autobiography.* Trans. Joseph Fabry
    and Judith Fabry. New York: Plenum, 1997.

Goldman, William. *The Princess Bride: S. Morgenstern's Classic Tale of True
    Love and High Adventure.* New York: Harcourt Brace Jovanovich,
    1973.

Goleman, Daniel. *Emotional Intelligence.* New York: Bantam Books, 1995.

Greenberger, Dennis, and Christine A. Padesky. *Mind over Mood: Change
    How You Feel by Changing the Way You Think.* New York: Guilford
    Press, 1995.

Griffith, Dean. Speech delivered to Aon Consulting, Eden Prairie,
    Minn., spring 1997.

Hesse, Hermann. *Magister Ludi: The Glass Bead Game.* New York:
    Bantam, 1980.

Hobson, J. Allan. *The Chemistry of Conscious States: How the Brain Changes
    Its Mind.* Boston: Little, Brown, 1994.

Kierkegaard, Søren. *Fear and Trembling, and the Sickness unto Death.*
    Garden City, N.Y.: Doubleday, 1954.

Kingsolver, Barbara. *High Tide in Tucson: Essays from Now or Never.* New
    York: Harper Collins, 1995.

Kunkel, Fritz. *Fritz Kunkel: Selected Writings.* Ed. John Sanford. Mahwah,
    N.J.: Paulist Press, 1984.

Lamott, Anne: *Bird by Bird: Some Instructions on Writing and Life.* New
    York: Parthenon, 1994.

Leider, Richard. *The Power of Purpose: Creating Meaning in Your Life and
    Work* . San Francisco: Berrett-Koehler, 1997.

Maslow, Abraham H. *The Farther Reaches of Human Nature.* New York:
    Viking, 1971.

Maultsby, Maxie. *Coping Better Anytime, Anywhere: The Handbook of
    Rational Self-Counseling.* New York: Simon & Schuster, 1987.

Ornstein, Robert E. *The Evolution of Consciousness: Of Darwin, Freud,
    and Cranial Fire: The Origins of the Way We Think.* New York:
    Prentice-Hall, 1991.

O'Toole, James. *Leading Change: Overcoming the Ideology of Comfort
    and the Tyranny of Custom.* San Francisco: Jossey-Bass, 1995.

Peck, M. Scott. *The Road Less Traveled: A New Psychology of Love,
    Traditional Values, and Spiritual Growth.* New York: Simon
    & Schuster, 1978.

"Prisoners of Silence." *Frontline*, program 1202. Produced by Jon Palfreman. Public Broadcasting System, October 19, 1993.

Russell, Mary Doria. *The Sparrow.* New York: Villard, 1996.

Ryan, Kathleen, and Daniel K. Oestreich. *Driving Fear Out of the Workplace: How to Overcome the Invisible Barriers to Quality, Productivity, and Innovation.* San Francisco: Jossey-Bass, 1991.

Schein, Edgar H. *Organizational Culture and Leadership: A Dynamic View.* 2nd ed. San Francisco: Jossey-Bass, 1992.

Sondheim, Stephen. "Sunday in the Park with George." Libretto. New York: RCA Records, 1994.

Uchitelle, Louis, and N. R. Kleinfield. "The Downsizing of America: On the Battlefield of Business, Millions of Casualties." *New York Times,* 3 March 1996, sec. 1, p. 1.

Watzlawick, Paul, Richard Fisch, and John N. Weakland. *Change: Principles of Problem Formation and Problem Resolution.* New York: W. W. Norton, 1974.

Wheatley, Margaret, and Myron Kellner-Rogers. *A Simpler Way.* San Francisco: Berrett-Koehler, 1996.

Wilson, Larry, and Hersch Wilson. *Changing the Game: The New Way to Sell.* New York: Simon & Schuster, 1986.

Wright, Robert. *The Moral Animal: Why We Are the Way We Are.* New York: Pantheon, 1994.

Index

ABC's practice in emergency rooms, 100–101

Absolutes in language, 115

Abundance, 157–158

Acceptance, 68, 198–199

Accountability, 60–61, 163–164, 230

Action statement of true self, 218–219

Adventure. *See also* Playing to Win

  barriers to, 6

  and cattle guard story, 4–6

  definition of, 3

  hero's journey, 125–132

  Keller on, 10

  life as, 10

  London Times ad, 6–7, 9–10

  South Pole expedition, 10

  spiritual adventure, 175–182

  surviving versus thriving, 10, 11

  thriving and, 10–15

  wilderness adventure, 225–228

Adventures of Alice in Wonderland, 211

Advertising, 30

Allison, John, 39, 65, 106, 189, 204–205

"Always" in language, 115

American HealthCorp, 93

Analysis paralysis, 136

Anger, 109–110, 117–118

Anxiety, 40. *See also* Fear

Aon Consulting, 33, 105, 163, 251

Argyris, Chris, 148, 152

Asimov, Isaac, 75

Autistic children, 63–65

Awful, meaning of, 24, 117

"Awful-worst fear" strategy, 136

Baseball, 200

Basketball, 72–73

BB&T, 39, 65, 106, 189, 204

Beliefs. *See also* Making stuff up (MSU)

  of children, 66

  mental maps and, 67–68

  about ourselves, 77

  and truths, 63–66

Bell Labs, 202

Best interests, 108–110

Big picture, 15

Bird by Bird (Lamott), 186

Blaming, 60–61, 152

Blanchard, Ken, xv–xvii

Boredom, 154

Brain

  irrational thinking and, 112

  and making stuff up, 71

  as perfect stupid servant, 112

  retraining of, for problem solving, 84–85, 89

Braslow, Alan, 47

Breathing technique, 96

British Airways, 157, 190
Bronowski, Jacob, 76
Brown, Juanita, 196
Buddha, 199
Burke, Tracy, 66, 95, 149

Calming and pausing, 95–97
Campbell, Don, 194–195
Campbell, Joseph, 126, 202
Campbell, Norma, 194–195
Cancer, 13
Carlson, Eric, 44
Cartography, 67
Castañeda, Carlos, 118–119
Catastrophizing, 104–105, 111–115
Cattle guards, 4–6, 77
Cause and effect, 51–52, 53
Centering, 96
Change
    ability to accomplish, 38–39
    fear of, 208
    and levels of commitment, 214
    planning for, 213–224
    in results, 52, 53, 59–60, 213
    steps in, 215–222
    Stop, Challenge, and Choose
        model, 213–214
Changing the Game, 45, 46–47
Chase Manhattan Bank, 189
Chemistry of Conscious States (Hobson),
    70
Children, 23–24, 66, 83–84, 109–110,
    112, 146, 194–195, 199–200, 202
Choice
    Castañeda on, 118–119
    and deeply prepared people,
        225–228
    definition of, 212
    for growth, 211–214
    and hero's journey, 125–132
    for integrity versus convenience,
        172
    and levels of commitment, 214
    life-defining choice, 171–172
    Maslow on, 134

"Name in the Pocket" game,
    133–138, 141
    and paradox of time, 229–230
    in Playing to Win, 26–28, 155–165,
        167–173
    power of, 230–231
    rational choices in Playing to Win,
        159–160
    Results Model, 59–60, 74, 75,
        163–164
    Stop, Challenge, and Choose
        model, 84–85, 89, 91–101, 105,
        113–114, 156, 171–172,
        213–214, 228–229
Christ, 199
Cigarran, Tom, 93
Closed mind, 151
Coca-Cola, 137–138
Comfort as goal of life, 152–153, 172
Comfort zone
    getting out of, 161–162
    staying in, 150–151
Comfortable being uncomfortable,
    26–28, 99
Commitment levels, 214
Competition
    and fear of failure, 143
    origin of term, 28
"Consensus hypnosis," 171
Control
    inability to control results, 50–51,
        53
    lack of control over life events, 59
    over thinking about life events,
        59–60
Convenience, 152–153, 172
Counselors, role of, 41–42
Courage
    and life shrinking/expanding, 226
    older people's wisdom on, 15–16
    in Playing to Win, 27–28
    and power of choice, 230–231
    and spirituality/maturity, 207–208
Creativity, 35

Cromwell, Oliver, 76
Crystal, John, 202–203

Dante, 154
David, Abbot, 179, 184
Dean, Dan, 105, 113
Death, 14, 175, 176
Deep breathing, 96
Deming, W. Edwards, 139–140
Dependence, 129–130
Depression, 154
Depression-fulfillment line, 32–33
Developmental journey. *See* Hero's
    journey
DiGiorgio, Sarah, 157
Discomfort. *See* Emotional
    discomfort
Diversification of interpretations,
    107–108
Dofasco Steel, 52, 159
Dragons in hero's journey, 128–132
Dreams, 177–179
Drunk driving, 152

Earhart, Amelia, 25
Ego
    dragon as, 129–132
    in dream of prince and master/
        servant ego, 177–179
    as "false self" in Kunkel's works,
        184–186
    fear and, 207–208
    reaction to hospitals, 185–186
Ego-centered dragon, and hero's
    journey, 129–132
Eighth-grade dance strategy, 136
Ellis, Albert, xxii, 40, 59
Emergency health care, 91–92,
    100–101, 186–187
Emotional cues, for Stop, Challenge,
    and Choose model, 93–94
Emotional discomfort
    comfortable being uncomfortable,
        26–28, 99
    fear of, 145–146

getting out of comfort zone,
    161–162
growth and, 26–28, 99
and staying in comfort zone,
    150–151
Emotional Intelligence (Goleman), 12
Emotional maturity
    acceptance of subjectivity and
        uncertainty, 75–76
    accountability for feelings and
        actions, 60–61
    and control over thinking about life
        events, 59–60
    definition of, 12–13
    mental maps and, 68
    and Playing to Win, 25
    Results Model and, 59–60, 74, 75,
        163–164
    Stop, Challenge, and Choose
        model, 171–172
    thinking clearly and, 38–40
    and thinking rationally, 105–110
    truth and, 65–68
Emotional resilience, 162–163
Emotions
    based on interpretation of events,
        55–60, 97–98
    "negative" emotions, 95
Empathic shift, 195–196
Employee loyalty, 85–89
Erickson, George A., 187
Eupsychia, xxi
Evolution of Consciousness (Ornstein), 71
Evolutionary psychology, 142
Excess, 175
Existential depression, 154

Facilitated communication (F/C),
    63–65
Failure. *See also* Winning and losing
    reframing of, as opportunity for
        growth, 44–47, 162–163
    thinking about, 42–47
    worry about, 42–44, 47
Fallible Human Being (FHB), 118

False Events Appearing Real, 132, 138
"False self," 184–186
Farther Reaches of Human Nature (Maslow), 123, 134, 184, 202
F/C (facilitated communication), 63–65
Fear
  avoidance of, 22–24
  of being wrong, 144
  of change, 208
  control management and, 140
  ego and, 207–208
  of emotional discomfort, 145–146
  of failure, 141, 143–144
  False Events Appearing Real, 132–138
  Four Fatal Fears, 138, 141–146, 149–150
  management's obligation concerning, 140
  and "Name in the Pocket" game, 133–138, 141
  needs and, 141–142
  of rejection, 145
  and spirituality/maturity, 207–208
  survival basis of, 140, 142
Feelings. *See* Emotional maturity; Emotions
FHB (Fallible Human Being), 118
Figgis, J. N., 126, 128
Flanagan, Tim, 99, 114–115
Follow your bliss, 202
Four Fatal Fears, 138, 141–146, 149–150
Frankl, Viktor, xxii, 31–33, 35, 43, 179, 180, 230–231
Fulfillment
  depression-fulfillment line, 32–33
  opportunities for, 35
  versus success, 32–35, 179–182
Future. *See* Planning

Gagan, Jamie, 91–92, 96
Gambling, 168–169

Games
  definition of, 19
  life as gamble, 168–169
  playing for survival, 24, 147–149
  Playing Not to Lose, 22–24, 47, 143–154, 167–173
  Playing to Win, 25–28, 35, 155–165, 167–173
  You Bet Your Life, 169, 173
General Motors, 74
Gibran, Kahlil, 206
GM. *See* General Motors
Goals, 160–161
Goleman, Daniel, 12, 94
Greenberger, Dennis, 58
Griffin, John, 27, 53
Griffith, Dean, 30
Griffith Laboratories, 30
Growing up. *See also* Emotional maturity; Spiritual maturity; Thinking clearly
  and choosing to thrive, 16–17
  courage and, 15–16
  emotional maturity, 12–13, 60–61
  and learning as rediscovery of what we already know, 14–15
  and making a difference, 16
  and seeing the big picture, 15
  spiritual maturity, 13–14
Growth. *See also* Change; Emotional maturity; Spiritual maturity
  choice of, 211–214
  life as, 157
  model of, 130
  price of, 171
  truths about, 127

Hahn, Kurt, xxii, 191
Hailey, Walter, 31–32, 39
Happiness, 35
Hegel, G. W. F., 65
Hero's journey
  dragons in, 128–132
  dragon's treasure in, 131–132
  ego-centered dragon and, 129–132

in *Return of the Jedi*, 129, 130
similarity of stories about, 125–129
theme running through stories of,
    125–129
and truths about growth, 127
Hierarchy of human needs, 123
High Tide in Tucson (Kingsolver), 198
Hobson, J. Allan, 70
Holocaust, 230–231
Hospitals
    ego's reaction to, 185–186
    emergency department in, 91–92,
        100–101
Human needs hierarchy, 123
Humanism, xx–xxi
Hunter-gatherer tribes, 142

"I can't," 116
"I don't want to hurt you" strategy,
    136
"I need," 116
Inconvenient versus awful, 117
Independence, 129–130
Inferno (Dante), 154
Inflammatory labeling, 117–118
Influence over results, 50–51, 53
Ingersoll, Robert, 146
Integrity, 172
Interdependence, 130
Interface America, Inc., 73
Interface Europe Ltd., 61
Interpretations of reality. *See also*
        Objective reality
    diversification of, 107–108
    feelings based on, 55–60, 97–98
    Playing Not to Lose, 149–150, 153,
        158, 170
    Playing to Win, 158, 164, 170
    Stop, Challenge, and Choose
        model, 84–85, 89, 91–101, 105,
        113–114
Involvement, 199–200
Irrational thinking
    absolutes in language, 115
    catastrophizing, 104–105, 111–115

and fear of failure, 46
inaccurate language and, 112–119
inflammatory labeling and,
    117–118
listening for, 118
Maultsby on, 40
Mini-Max technique for, 114–115
and Playing Not to Lose, 151
saying "awful," 24, 117
and saying "I can't," 116
saying "I need," 116

Judging, 197
Jung, Carl, 178, 190–191

Kearns, Jim, 101
Keller, Helen, 10
Kellner-Rogers, Myron, 158
Kelly, Paul, 202
Kelly, Ruth, 202
Kierkegaard, Søren, 163
Kingsolver, Barbara, 198
Knapp, Rob, 51, 160
Kunkel, Fritz, 14, 178, 179, 180, 181,
    184

Labeling as inflammatory, 117–118
Lamott, Anne, 186
Language
    absolutes in, 115
    "awful," 24, 117
    catastrophizing, 104–105, 111–115
    "I can't," 116
    "I need," 116
    inaccurate language and irrational
        thinking, 112–119
    inconvenient versus awful, 117
    inflammatory labeling, 117–118
    listening for inaccurate language,
        118
    objective reality and, 118
Learning, as rediscovery of what we
    already know, 14–15
Legends. *See* Hero's journey
Leider, Dick, 15–16, 24, 130, 205, 214

Levels of commitment, 214
Listening, in understanding exercise, 196–197
Little League, 200
London Times, 6–7, 9–10
Losing. *See* Winning and losing
Love
   doing what you love or loving what you do, 206–207
   Frankl on, 35
   and fulfillment, 35
   and service, 193–200
Loyalty of employees, 85–89
Lund, Pug, 43–44

Making stuff up (MSU)
   about others, 77
   about ourselves, 76–77
   acceptance of subjectivity and uncertainty, 75–76
   brain function and, 71
   at General Motors, 74
   and incomplete and inaccurate mental maps, 69–71
   "larger picture" and, 76
   and organizations of people, 72–73
   women's basketball and, 72–73
   at work, 73, 75
Management, fear used by, 140
Man's Search for Meaning (Frankl), 31, 43, 230–231
Maps and mapmakers, 67–68
Marshall, John, 52, 159
Martin Engineering, 113
Maryland state government, 27, 53
Maslow, Abraham, xx–xxi, xxii, 45, 122–123, 134, 138, 140, 173, 184, 202
Maslow's pyramid, 123
Mass Mutual, 99, 114–115
Maturity. *See* Emotional maturity; Growing up; Spiritual maturity; Thinking clearly
Maultsby, Maxie, xxii, 24, 37, 39–40, 42, 59, 108, 112

McLuhan, Marshall, 151
"Me to we" shift, 14, 186–191, 195–196
Mencken, H. L., 79
Mental maps
   and beliefs and truths, 67–68, 72
   best interests for, 108–110
   at General Motors, 74
   of human organizations, 72
   and making stuff up, 69–71
   "no trust," 149
   and Playing Not to Lose, 150–152, 153, 170
   for Playing to Win, 157–158, 164, 170
   scarcity, 149
Merrill Lynch, 51, 160
Metacognition. *See* Thinking about thinking
Mills, Helen, 33, 163
Mind over Mood (Greenberger and Padesky), 58
Mini-Max technique, 114–115
Monthei, Kathy, 45
Moral Animal (Wright), 142
MSU. *See* Making stuff up (MSU)
Myths. *See* Hero's journey

"Name in the Pocket" game, 133–138, 141
Needs, 116, 141–142
Needs hierarchy, 123
"Never" in language, 115
Nin, Anïas, 226

Objective reality
   definition of, 105–107
   diversification of interpretations, 107–108
   language and, 118
   of needs, 141
   in Playing to Win, 159
   thinking with best interests in mind, 108–110
Obstacles and planning, 222

Of Death and the Fear of Dying (Smith), 172
ORION Learning, 22, 85, 97, 162
Ornstein, Robert E., 71
Ortega y Gasset, José, 228
O'Toole, James, 74
Outdoor Adventure Course, 85
Outward Bound, 191
Overcoming Organizational Defenses (Argyris), 148

Padesky, Christine, 58
Painted cattle guards. *See* Cattle guards
Paradox of time, 229–230
Parents, 109–110, 112, 146, 179–182, 190, 199–200, 202
Peck, Scott, 77
Pecos Monastery, 179, 184
Pecos River Change Management, xvi, xxi–xxiv, 249–251
Pecos River Learning and Conference Center, 45, 117, 180–181, 194, 196, 218
Perception, and making stuff up, 71
Persistence
    competition and, 143
    and Stop, Challenge, and Choose model, 224
    thinking about, 44–45
Personal best, 160–161
Personal vision statement, 219–221
Peterson, Edwin, 113
Planning
    action statement of true self, 218–219
    creating your plan, 221–222
    and levels of commitment, 214
    need for, 213–214
    obstacles and support identified, 222
    purpose statement, 218–219
    refining your plan, 223
    sharing your plan, 223
    steps in, 215–222
    and Stop, Challenge, and Choose model, 224

strategies and, 221
tactics and, 221–222
talents identified, 217
using your plan, 223–224
values identified, 216–217
vision statement, 219–221
Plato, 14
Playing for survival, 24, 147–149
Playing Not to Lose, 22–24, 47, 143–154, 158, 167–173
Playing to Win. *See also* Success; Winning and losing
    and ability to be comfortable being uncomfortable, 26–28
    abundance and, 157–158
    accountability and, 163–164
    choice for integrity versus convenience, 172
    as conscious choice, 26–28
    definition of, 25, 35
    epitaph for, 155
    failure as learning and growth, 162–163
    getting out of comfort zone, 161–162
    interpretation of reality in, 158, 164, 170
    and life as growth, 157
    mental maps for, 157–158, 164, 170
    personal best and, 160–161
    philosophy of, 157, 164, 170
    rational choices in, 159–160
    rationale for, 165
    responses for, 158–164, 164, 170
    results from, 167–173
    and Stop, Challenge, and Choose, 156, 171–172
    trust and, 157–158
    truth based on objective reality, 159
Power of Purpose (Leider), 15–16, 130
Prepared people, 225–228
Problem solving
    and belief that we shouldn't have problems, 80–81
    complex problems, 79

in emergency rooms, 91–92,
100–101
and retraining the brain, 84–85
Stop, Challenge, and Choose
model, 84–85, 89, 91–101, 105
unions at Coca-Cola plant, 85–89,
97–98, 99
Purpose statement, 216–217

Rational Behavior Therapy (RBT), 40
Rational thinking, 105–110, 159–160.
See also Thinking clearly
RBT (Rational Behavior Therapy), 40
Reality. *See also* Interpretations of real-
ity
best interests for, 108–110
dedication to, 71
diversification of interpretations of,
107–108
of needs, 141
objective reality, 105–107
truth based on objective reality in
Playing to Win, 159
Reframing of failure, 44–47, 162–163
Regan, Bart, 178–179
Rejection, fear of, 145
Relationships. *See* Love
Relaxation, 96
Relief as goal of life, 152–153
Resilience, 162–163
Results
and cause and effect, 51–52, 53
change in, 52, 53, 59–60
inability to control, 50–51, 53
influence over, 50–51, 53, 212–213
and Playing Not to Lose, 167–173
and Playing to Win, 167–173
Results Model, 59–60, 74, 75,
163–164
rules of, 50–53
at work, 73–75
Results Model, 59–60, 74, 75, 163–164
Return of the Jedi, 129, 130
Risk taking, and Playing to Win,
26–28

Road Less Traveled (Peck), 77
Robbins, Tom, 196
Rogers, Carl, xxi
Root, Bob, 97, 162
Rosen, Rachel, 190
Ruane, Paul, 150
Russell, Bertrand, 6
Russell, Mary Doria, 171

Sandburg, Carl, 164
Sangre de Cristo Mountains, 225–228
Sayre, Woodrow Wilson, 161
Scarcity, 149
Schering-Plough HealthCare, 150
Science, 76
Self
action statement of true self,
218–219
expression of true self, 201–208
"false self," 184–186
true self versus ego, 184–187
Self-actualization, xxi, 123, 184, 202
Self-awareness, 94, 95–97
Self-promotion, 150, 152
Self-protection, 150, 152
Service, 193–200
Shackleton, Sir Ernest, 10
Shakespeare, William, 57–58
Sheehan, George, 161
Siddhartha, 199
Simpler Way (Wheatley and Kellner-
Rogers), 158
Smith, Alexander, 172
Snakes, 55–57, 58
SOAR, 159
Soccer, 84, 89
Sondheim, Stephen, 161
South Pole expedition, 10
Sparrow (Russell), 171
Spiritual maturity
acceptance, 198–199
in business world, 187–189
death and, 14, 175, 176
definition of, 14, 183–184
and doing important work, 204–206

doing what you love or loving what
    you do, 206–207
and dream of prince and
    master/servant ego, 177–179
empathic shift, 195–196
expression of true self, 201–208
fear and, 207–208
involvement, 199–200
loving service, 193–200
"me to we" shift, 14, 186–191,
    195–196
questions central to, 13–14,
    176–182, 208
spiritual adventure, 175–182
and success versus fulfillment,
    179–182
talents and, 201–206
true self versus ego, 184–187
understanding, 196–197
and unfolding your wings, 189–191
Sports. *See* Baseball; Basketball; Soccer
Steele, Wendy, 22, 85–89, 137–138
Stop, Challenge, and Choose model,
    84–85, 89, 91–101, 105, 113–114,
    156, 171–172, 213–214, 224,
    228–229
Storytelling, 70
STPs (Strategic Thinking Processes),
    46–47
Strategic Thinking Processes (STPs),
    46–47
Strategies and planning, 221
Subjectivity. *See* Making stuff up
    (MSU)
Success. *See also* Playing to Win;
    Winning and losing
beyond success, 34–35
and depression-fulfillment line,
    32–33
and feeling bad, 30–34
requirements for, 35
rethinking success, 30–35
traditional definition of, 29–34, 35
versus fulfillment, 32–35, 179–182
versus happiness, 35

Suffering, 35, 43, 163
Sunday in the Park with George,
    161–162
Support and planning, 222
Survival
fear and, 140, 142
playing for survival, 24, 147–149
versus thriving, 10, 11

Tactics and planning, 221–222
Talents
definition of, 217
and doing important work,
    205–206
identification of, 217
use of, 201–204
"Teaching Smart People How to
    Learn" (Argyris), 152
"Thank God" strategy, 136
Thinking. *See also* Making stuff up
    (MSU)
closed mind, 151
feelings based on interpretation of
    events, 55–60, 97–98
tragic flaw in, 57–59
Thinking about thinking
on failure, 42–47
Maultsby on, 37, 42
on persistence, 44–45
practical example of, 42–45
Thinking clearly. *See also* Problem
    solving
with best interests in mind,
    108–110
and control over thinking about life
    events, 59–60
importance of, for emotional
    maturity, 38–40
Maultsby's legacy for, 40
mental maps and, 67–68
about results, 49–53
Stop, Challenge, and Choose
    model, 84–85, 89, 91–101, 105,
    113–114, 156, 171–172

Strategic Thinking Processes
(STPs), 46–47
truths and beliefs, 63–68
Thinking rationally, 105–110, 159–160
Thriving
choosing to thrive, 16–17
courage and, 15–16
emotional maturity and, 12–13
and learning as rediscovery of what
we already know, 14–15
and making a difference, 16
and seeing the big picture, 15
spiritual maturity and, 13–14
surviving versus, 10, 11
"Wellness" program, 10–11
Time, paradox of, 229–230
Tragic flaw, 57–59
Treasure of the dragon, 131–132
Triage, 92
True self
action statement of, 218–219
expression of, 201–208
versus ego, 184–187
Trust
"no trust" perspective, 149
in Playing to Win, 157–158
Truths. *See also* Making stuff up
(MSU)
based on objective reality in
Playing to Win, 159
beliefs and, 63–66
definition of, 66
mental maps and, 67–68, 72
"the truth" used in language, 115

Uncertainty. *See* Making stuff up
(MSU)
Understanding, 196–197
Unfolding your wings, 189–191
Unionization, 85–89
U-turn strategy, 136

Values
definition of, 216
identification of, 216–217

Vietnamese children, 194–195
Vision statement, 219–221

Walker, John, 61
Weather and prepared people,
225–228
Weisman, Billy, 35, 159
Weisman Enterprises, Inc., 35, 159
Wellness Program, 10–11, 38–40
Wells, H. G., 175
Wheatley, Margaret, 158
Whitener, Gordon, 73
Whole Systems Associates, 196
Wilde, Oscar, 163
Wilderness adventure, 225–228
Wilson, Hersch, xiii
Wilson, Larry
biographical information on, xiii
Blanchard on, xv–xvii
and dream about prince and his
master/servant ego, 177–179
early career of, 42–45
family of, 179–182
on genesis of book, xix–xxii
Wilson Learning Corporation, xxi,
10–11, 45, 249
Winning and losing. *See also* Success
playing for survival, 24, 147–149
Playing Not to Lose, 22–24, 47,
143–154, 158, 167–173
Playing to Win, 25–28, 35,
155–165, 167–173
redefining, 20–28
Wizard of Oz, 131
Women's basketball, 72–73
Worry
as cause of illness, 40
about failure, 42–44, 47
Wright, Robert, 142

You Bet Your Life, 169, 173

Zorba the Greek, 81, 229

CONTACTING LARRY WILSON OR PECOS RIVER

Larry Wilson
If you would like to have more information about speeches and workshops by Larry Wilson, leave questions for the authors, or discuss **Playing to Win**® in the workplace and in life, please visit the author's web sites at:

www.larrywilson.com

and

thegreatgameoflife.com.

Pecos River
Pecos River® is a division of Aon Consulting Worldwide, with offices in North America, Europe, and Asia. For more information about Pecos River® and its consulting and training services, please contact it at:

Pecos River® Division Aon Consulting, Inc.
US Phone: 1-800-PecosRiver
www.pecosriver.com

For additional copies of
PLAY TO WIN!
Choosing Growth over Fear in Work and Life
visit your favorite bookstore
or contact
Larry Wilson & Associates
941/964-3017
or larry@thegreatgameoflife.com